30 DAILY DEVOTIONS FOR

BATTLE-WEARY PARENTS

A SCRIPTURE-BASED GUIDE FOR
PARENTING IN THE TRENCHES

PAM
PARISH

FOREWORD BY COLLEEN ROUSE

PRAISE FOR *BATTLE-WEARY PARENTS*

A 30-Day Devotional Guide for Parenting in the Trenches

"Don't fear the trial that sits before you. Trust in the God who knows all things, created all things, and promises that all things will work together for your good. He is sustaining you." This is one of the many insights and truths that Pam so beautifully lays out for the weary foster or adoptive parent. While foster care and adoption journeys are full of joys and triumphs, there are also those days when the fear of failure is lurking around the corner. Thank you, Pam, for yet another incredible resource that is like a balm for the heart of parents who are loving on kids from hard places.

Andy and Sandra Stanley, *North Point Community Church*

Little on earth is as physically, emotionally and spiritually exhausting as nurturing a wounded child toward health. It can bring unparalleled rewards, too. But the deep and omnipresent needs can be taxing beyond what any ministry outside the home demands. Yes, we chose this. But, as with most any great undertaking, we likely grasped only a fraction of all that would be involved when we started. Mere duty or idealistic hopes will not sustain us for the long-haul. Drawing deep from the riches of Scripture and the real heartache and joy of her own journey, Pam Parish prepares us to persevere in love. Ultimately, she helps us drink deep from the one Source that can sustain us through the dark places and murky swamps: the God who has loved us beyond all calculation or logic, drawing us – and the precious lives in our charge – to His tender care.

Jedd Medefind, President of the *Christian Alliance for Orphans* **and author of** *Becoming Home*

I LOVE this. For so many reasons, I really do. The first being that it addresses our hearts and thought lives. This is where I see in my own life, and the other foster and adoptive parents around me, roots of bitterness grow. If we are not careful, we go from weary parents to bitter parents because we fail to look at who GOD says He is in the situations and lives of these kids. By taking us back to The Word, Pam helps us to gain the right perspective, refocus and love out of His strength and not our own.

Whitney Bunker, Founder & Executive Director of *A City Without Orphans*

I read the devotional through a critical lens. Over the last 30 years working in foster care and adoption, I have walked with many families through some horrifically dark moments, some which lead to disruption or dissolution of the adoption. I felt sure I would read passages in Battle Weary that would make me cringe, that would make me angry, that would make my heart, as an adoptee, hurt for the children you would refer to, and would leave me wanting to write things from the child's perspective. I read and re-read each day, recalling and reflecting on the parents and children I have had the joy and pain of walking with through their journey. In the end, I wish I had this devotional to give them as they began to tell me how their experiences are shaping and changing their family—often in the direction they did not wish to go.

I loved many parts of the book but there was one paragraph that summed up all that I've wanted to say over the years but couldn't, for many reasons. "Precious moms and dads, there is no diagnosis- no RAD, no ADHD, no Bipolar, no Borderline Personality Disorder, no FAS, no ANYTHING—in which the Lord can't bring peace, understanding and victory. There is also no crisis—no runaway, no drug addicted teen, no sexually active teen, no pregnant teen, no violent outbursts, no rejection, no arrest, no ANYTHING—in which the Lord can't intervene and restore. Trust in Him for wisdom, lean on Him for understanding, allow Him to direct your steps and rely on Him for mercy, grace and patience in your journey." These words alone bring healing to the heart of a child who has longed to feel accepted, longed to feel in relationship with others, and yet is blamed for the distrust and walls they have built to protect themselves as a result of wounds inflicted upon them by this world.

Pam has written an amazing devotional that could only be written by someone who has (and still is) walking the walk. I love her heart and I loved each word from her heart on each page. God has given Pam an amazing gift, I am so grateful to her for taking His gift and pouring it out for all of those who are hurting.

Amy Curtis, Director of Post Adoption & Counseling for *Buckner International & Maternity Services*

We don't like to think that, as parents, we can become "battle-weary." The truth is that we do. Pam again captures the heart needs of adoptive and foster parents in this 2nd book in the *Ready or Not* series. Her transparency regarding her own experiences offers rich credibility to the journey she leads her readers through. I highly recommend this study for every foster or adoptive family, whether they're already battle-weary or just starting out.

Jayne Schooler, Child Development Specialist, Back2Back, Author

Battle-Weary Parents

30 Daily Devotions

A Scripture-based Guide for Parenting in the Trenches

Written By:

Pam Parish

Foreword By:

Colleen Rouse

Editor: Mallory Cruz
Cover Art: Big Stock Photography
Cover Design: German Creative
Author Photo: Craig Obrist Photography
Inspiration: Every foster and adoptive family that I've ever met.

ISBN: 0996492895
ISBN-13: 978-0-9964928-9-8

DEDICATION

To every foster and adoptive parent in the trenches with children whose lives have been shattered in ways we can hardly imagine. Your commitment and love are extraordinary; thank you for living your redeeming stories.

Pam Parish

CONTENTS

ACKNOWLEDGMENTS

Throughout the writing of this devotional, my friends have often heard me say, "I'm having to live almost every single day of this writing." It's true. The Lord literally walked me through the very real emotions laid out on these pages and taught me how to trust Him in the midst of my sorrows and fears. In everything, there was never a day that I walked alone. More than any other person on this planet, I want to acknowledge the one who is by my side in every moment, the absolute love of my life, my husband, Steve. Regardless of the circumstance, he has remained my ever-present shoulder to cry on, a gentle voice of encouragement and faithful voice of wisdom. Steve, I am more in love with you today than I could have ever imagined in my sixteen year-old mind when I met you. Thank you for loving me well.

To our daughters, grand-children and new son-in-law—Katya, Kelsey, Seara, Elizabeth, Charlie, Kristan, Heather, Juan, Jayden, Adrianna, Junior and Tyree—I love you so much. You make my life full and I'm honored that you call me mom and Nana. Thank you for loving me even when I try to do the stanky legg, whip and nae nae, when I sing out loud, upload embarrassing pictures to Instagram and yell at the TV during a football game. That's unconditional love. You guys are my life. I am the woman, the daughter of God, that I am today because you've taught me how to love well, listen fully, embrace my imperfections and accept grace because you've given it to me freely.

To our parents'—Gary & Janice Parish, Wayne Gary, Janice Smith, Yvonne Marcus—and all of our extended family: thank you for praying for our family regularly and for loving us. I'm so grateful for your understanding, your wisdom, and your encouragement along the way.

To everyone who participated in this book coming to pass, thank you. Dennis & Colleen Rouse, your influence in our lives goes far beyond simply being our pastors. You are family to us, and to all of our girls. Thank you for always walking alongside us with grace, understanding, mercy and wisdom. Colleen, thank you for being gracious enough to write the Foreword to this book. Your words honored and blessed me. Beth Templeton, I'm ever so grateful that you came into my life as a friend and fellow traveler in this journey of adoption. Thank you for writing the Afterword; your words will be balm to the soul of countless foster and adoptive families. Andrew & Michele Schneidler, I'm so thankful that you shared The Plate Exercise with the readers of this book. The experience of The Refresh Conference and The Plate Exercise are forever engraved on me—what a powerful and life-changing moment that was for me. Your friendship is precious to me. Mallory Cruz, there are few words that are appropriate enough to describe who you are to me. I know you disagree when I say it, but the only word that I can think of is this—hero. Your friendship means the world to me. I've learned how to struggle gracefully and with joy as I've walked through life with you. Thank you for taking time out of your life to edit the pages of this book. Enduring my addiction to commas, ellipsis and lists of three is a very commendable act of patience. I love you. Ty Buckingham, thank you for working with me through the process of cover design. Your input was invaluable as we walked through the many options for not just the cover design for this book, but the series as it continues. I appreciate you more than you know.

There is absolutely no way that our family would have made it through all that we have without having an incredible community of friends who "get it." To all of my friends in the foster care and adoption community, I am astounded that I get to walk this journey with you. Your stories, your input into my story and the collective of our children's stories is a tapestry of beauty and grace that only Jesus could craft. There are so many things that I could say to each of you individually about how you've impacted my life in significant ways, but that would be a book in and of itself. So, know that even though I only have space for your names, you are so much more to me than what any few characters on a page could articulate. Maridel Sandberg, Kevin & Lesli Reece, Andy & Sandra Stanley, Mark & Tona Ottinger, Tara Bradford, Lynn & Ruby Johnston, Daniel & Whitney Bunker, Jedd Medefind, Elizabeth Weibe, David & Lisa Hennessey, David & Jayne Schooler, Amy Curtis, Susan Williams, the entire Buckner team, Andy Cook, Ty & Kristen Bryant, Tracy Baird, Frank & Johnna Stein, Denise Cox, Tim & Amy Rider, John & Deena Theiss, Paul & Janice McClean, Lisa Ferris Johnson, Andrea Pierce Young, Ben & Virginia Bubar, Jason & Dawn Wright, Russell & Lisa Qualls, Katie Gonzalez, Ernie & Cheryl Johnson, Susan Linebarger, Stephanie Fast, Kelly Clayton Berry, Amy Huston Callahan, Michael & Amy Monroe, Carissa Woodwyk, Carol Kochon, Ryan & Crystal Casey, Wendy Willard, Jameel & Makini Peters, Kalina D'Orazio, Scott & Jessica Torres, Kathleen Hamer, Kelly Rosati, Meg Meeker, Ryan Dobson, Ed Schermerhorn, Catie Finley Lumpkin, Tracy Whitt, Jennifer Summers, Randy Doleman, Heath Pressley, Herbie Newell, Carrie Swanson-Blake, Sam & Maria Hansen-Quine, Mary Ostyn, Johnston Moore, Paul & Kristin Hastings Wright, Emily Davidson, Nicole Tabor, Miki Hall Skelton, Claudia Flye Fletcher, Susan Hillis, Jordan Palser, Jessica Choi, Millie Snook, Betsy Lewis, Alex & Bonnie Menoni, Toni Esparza, Karen Springs, Jen Schneider, Jason Weber, Jason Johnson, Ty & Macy Richardson, Chad & Laurie Clinger, Randy & Kimberly Gebele

It is the privilege of my life that God has granted me the honor of launching an organization like Connections Homes which takes part of our family's story and makes it reality for other families who desire to step into the story of a young adult who has no one else. To the team of people who surround me in this vision, I can't thank you enough. You take my small ideas and make them big. You see the vision and believe in it with me. Your contributions are priceless. Catharine Jordan, Seara Smith, Kali Skar, Andrie Baker, Lori McCune, Lisa Hennessey, Chrissy Strohmeyer, Gary Walderich, Mindy Park, Kevin & Lesli Reece, Sayu Abend, Gregg Pawlowski, Rob & Dawn McCleland, Daniel & Julie Homrich, Debra Potter, Laura Engelbrecht, Mary Frances Bowley, Aaron, Ebony, Amirah, Gigi and all of our Connections Homes families.

Finally, to our incredibly amazing community of friends and family. Life is more enjoyable because of you. Your friendship, prayers, and support of our family makes the day-to-day of our journey easier. We absolutely love doing life with you. Hondo & Becky Clayton, Patrick & Seth Gullett, Steven Gary, Crystal Tanner, Austin Ferguson, Wendy Gary, Shelby Gary, Brandon Gary, Brenda & Jerry Miller, Danny Miller, Brian & Lisa Miller, Nathan & Laura Miller, Nathanial & Stephanie Miller, Skeet & Jenn West, Gary & Paula Walderich, George & Debbie Stull, Chrissy Strohmeyer, Chuck & Sherry Gozder, Kyle & Mallory Cruz, Kyle & Jessica Purintun, Nathan & Ashley Williams, Charlie & Erin Pike, Chad & Beth Whiteside, Montell & Kristin Jordan, Glenn & Taylor Scott, Alan CeCe, Ronne Rock, Ryan & Christi Howard, Jeremy & Emily Hopwood, David & Amber Stephens, Avery & Dede Nesbitt, Charles & Kristin Santa Maria, Terry & Linda Nash, Ross & Kelly Coker, Stephanie Jensen.

BE STRONG AND COURAGEOUS, DO NOT BE AFRAID OR TREMBLE AT THEM, FOR
THE LORD YOUR GOD IS THE ONE WHO GOES WITH YOU HE WILL NOT FAIL YOU
OR FORSAKE YOU.

DEUTERONOMY 31:6

INTRODUCTION

A soldier is never *ready* for war. They're simply faithful to the call to defend their country. Despite their fears, despite the comfort of home, despite their preference—they go. When you enlisted as a foster/adoptive parent, you also signed up for a war: a very real, gritty, long, and sometimes exhausting battle for the heart, mind, and healing of your child.

Ready or not...

The term *battle weary* is often used to describe a type of fatigue felt by soldiers when they get tired of fighting in a war. This type of fatigue leads to depression, anxiety, exhaustion, and other forms of mental anguish. It's an overwhelming feeling of hopelessness that the battle is never going to end, and you simply don't feel like fighting another day. As a parent of children from hard places, I have often found myself there. Weary, worn-out, and desperate for a break or breakthrough in the war for my children's lives.

My first experience with battle weariness as a parent started one fall afternoon when our sixteen-year-old daughter didn't come home from school. This particular daughter was sweet, loving, kind, and gentle. She was also secretive, deceptive, and sneaky. We used everything from keystroke recorders to phone parental controls to try and keep her safe and guide her. None of it mattered. Her desire to control her own life was more powerful than anything we could muster up in our parenting toolbox.

After a couple of hours of trying to locate her through friends, we made the dreaded phone call to police to report our daughter missing—a runaway. Little did I know that this day would set into motion a course of events that would result in her being found, running away again, being placed in a residential treatment facility for troubled teenagers, and eventually returning to live with her biological family. Talk about feeling like a failure. It was a season of time marked with miles and miles of prayers and tears during long road trips to visit her. Time and time again, I questioned myself, our decision to adopt, our abilities as parents, and God. How could it *really* be this bad? I **know** God spoke to us about *this* child.

In the years since, I've found myself at this place on many occasions for different reasons and different children. I've also heard the feeling repeated by parent after parent, as the struggle to keep their head above water in parenting children with such deep emotional scars and behavioral patterns continues. Every day is a battle, and it seems like they will never again experience life with happiness. "But I have **faith**!" "But God **told** me to do this." "But, I cover them in prayer **every** day."

I understand. Those are all the same things I said to myself and screamed at God when I was overwhelmed and distraught in the midst of the battle. On those long days and dark nights when it seemed all hope was lost, no one understood, and I was all alone in this fight, I did the only thing that I knew to do. I reached with all my might for the last thread of faith that I could muster and cried out to God to help me make it. And He did.

There is no darker place than the depths of a broken heart full of fear, regret, doubt, and failure. Yet, it's in that very dark place that God meets us and shines His light brightly. It doesn't matter the size of the room or the depth of the darkness—a single match can bring light. Sometimes, in our journey as parents of children from hard places, all we need is a single spark of hope to help us keep going.

In the next 30 days, my prayer is that you find your spark of hope.

The truth of our journey with Christ is that even in the very center of God's will for our lives, we can face our toughest battles. That child we prayed for or are helping out of a bad situation, the one we dreamed about and were promised—yes, *that* very child will create scars on our knees from hours spent in prayer.

In the midst of the storm, it rarely sprinkles; most often, it pours. Sometimes the only way to survive is to drop your umbrella and dance in the rain. In the middle of my storms, I've discovered that the things God promises us are the very things the enemy tries to steal with every weapon from hell. This, friends, is war.

Ready or not…

~Pam Parish~

Discussion Questions – Introduction

1. Have you ever considered the healing of your child's heart and mind to be a spiritual war? Does this understanding change anything for you? If so, what?

2. As this study begins, Pam encourages you that the darkest places in life are where the light shines the brightest. Why do you think she says this? What do you hope to discover over the next 30-days?

3. Read Psalm 73:26. What does it mean for your flesh and heart to fail? How does it make you feel to think of God as "the strength of your heart and portion forever?"

4. What are you specifically asking God to do in your heart and family? How can this group pray for you?

HOW TO USE THIS 30-DAY JOURNAL

TOGETHER

I've written this journal with couples and friends in mind because any journey is easier when there's someone else linking arms with you. If you're married, walk through the thirty days with your spouse. If you're a single parent, find a trusted friend who will challenge you, encourage you, and who isn't afraid to help you dig deep for the truth. You are going to need to rely on each other in your journey. Start now.

REPEATED THEMES

Although no two days of this study are exactly the same, you will see some repeated themes as we travel through the next thirty days. God's mandates regarding the orphan are repeated often in the Bible, so we will revisit them again and again. There are also common areas that cause families to falter and stall. I will repeat them in different ways to make sure you're thinking through potential challenges from every possible angle.

SCRIPTURE STUDY

Each day of *Ready or Not* includes a main scripture and scripture meditations. I encourage you to write down these verses in your personal journal and take time to meditate on them throughout the day. If there's one thing that's most important in this journey, it's the Word written on your heart so you remember it in difficult times. The Word will sustain you, encourage you, give you insight, and bring life and joy into your home. Take all the time you need to meditate on it so it roots deeply into your heart.

JOURNALING

You are going to experience a wide range of emotions, victories, and setbacks. Journaling is a great way to remember and celebrate God's faithfulness. You'll sometimes feel like you're *never* going to get through this challenge or *this* behavior is never going to end, but you will and they do. Being able to look back at the difficulties you've overcome will bring immense encouragement as you move forward.

PRAYER STARTERS

I've given you short prayer starters at the end of each day. These are simply my words—nothing special or sacred. Make them your own. Talk to God about the real stuff that's happening in your heart. This journey is an ongoing conversation between you and God. Be real. Be you. He knows anyway.

DISCUSSION QUESTIONS

At the end of each day, you'll find a set of questions designed to help you work through and apply the day's devotion. These can be discussed as a couple, in a small group setting, or with a trusted friend. I encourage you to take the time to discuss this material with someone else.

Place these words on your hearts. Get them deep inside you. Tie them on your hands and foreheads as a reminder. Teach them to your children. Talk about them wherever you are, sitting at home or walking in the street; talk about them from the time you get up in the morning until you fall into bed at night. Inscribe them on the doorposts and gates of your cities so that you'll live a long time, and your children with you, on the soil that God promised to give your ancestors for as long as there is a sky over the earth.

Deuteronomy 11:18-21 (MSG)

FOREWORD

That's absolutely wonderful or that's absolutely preposterous.

This is the range of response a perspective adoptive parent receives from friends and loved ones when they propose the idea of opening their home to embrace a new family member. The truth is that those of us who have never adopted have no idea how to support those who step into this unique parenting role, particularly if the children are school age and older. Such parents are both courageous, unselfish, and certainly few in number. We admire them, and pray for them and now fortunately we can add value to them by placing into their hands a specific resource designed help them enjoy greater success in navigating parental challenges.

My husband, Dennis, and I have witnessed Pam and her husband, Steve, open their home to not one but six young women, each with their unique personalities and backgrounds. We have prayed together, cried together and rejoiced together while watching them face and manage the oftentimes complex issues that presented themselves in the lives of these beautiful girls. This devotional is a product of their discoveries along the way. Pam writes from a place of honesty and transparency, which makes her book a powerful companion. She has chosen to address the raw and real issues associated with this unique role of parenting which places her writing in the essential-to-life category. Her insight is rooted in Scripture which, as the ultimate authority, has the power to transform us like no other literature. She provides opportunity for valuable introspection and a means to discover, challenge and exchange faulty thoughts with Truth. The reader is invited to approach and address the battles they may be facing in such a way to turn weariness into readiness, discouragement to inspiration, and despair into enjoyment. The fact that all of this is presented in a devotional format is extremely beneficial in helping foster and adoptive parents with great insight on a daily basis.

I foresee *Ready or Not for Battle-Weary Parents* being a game-changer for many parents and relationships. It will be much more than another book to gather dust on a shelf. Rather, I see the corners of many pages bent and the cover showing the signs of wear and tear as it becomes an often read (and re-read) source of life to the parents who discover the victory inscribed on its pages.

Colleen Rouse

PREFACE

When I was 9 I stole my dad's credit card. There, I said it.

I had clicked on an ad for Revitalize meal-replacement shakes. They were willing to let you try their product for free with a subscription to their program, which sent you new shakes on a regular basis. They needed a credit card number for the subscription. So I borrowed my dad's without permission.

My dad is a creature of habit, so I knew where to look for his wallet. I took out just one card (in case he came to look for his wallet while I was still gone) and went back to my computer. I filled out the form, being sure to use my dad's name to avoid getting caught, and typed in the card number, expiry date, and CVC. Then I replaced the card, careful to leave the wallet exactly as I found it, and went about my day.

I was guilty of theft, fraud, and deception. And my parents had every right to ground me for life. They were the victims of my misbehavior, and I wronged them. But I was hurting, too.

See, what most parents miss in situations similar to this one is that the offender isn't *trying* to be offensive. I was hurting. I was deeply insecure. I had no friends, I felt lonely and fat, and I reasoned that getting skinnier could make me more popular.

Does that make what I did right? Absolutely not. I did get in trouble, but my parents understood that I hadn't taken my dad's credit card just to steal from him. I did it in an effort to fix my own problems.

When a car gets stuck in a muddy ditch, those closest to it often get splattered. What my mom has written is a guide to help you catch your breath. It's a reminder that we are not trying to hurt you or make your life more messy. We're just stuck.

Kristan Faith Parish

I WAITED PATIENTLY FOR THE LORD TO HELP ME, AND HE TURNED TO ME AND HEARD MY CRY. HE LIFTED ME OUT OF THE PIT OF DESPAIR, OUT OF THE MUD AND THE MIRE. HE SET MY FEET ON SOLID GROUND AND STEADIED ME AS I WALKED ALONG.

PSALMS 40:1-3

DAY 1: YOUR HELP COMES FROM THE LORD

Coming down from the initial placement high can feel like you've fallen off a cliff or have been hit by a fast-moving train. It happens in an instant, one day you're sailing along thinking, "They were all wrong this foster/adoption thing is awesome!" Then BAM! You wonder if someone snuck in and switched your kid with a look-alike from another planet. Or, you wonder if everyone lied about the honeymoon. What honeymoon? This kid declared war the moment he moved into his new bedroom! Either way, we all arrive at this place in our journey wondering why we signed up for this, how we're going to make it through it, and how long it's going to last. No, really, how long is this going to last?

Recently I read a quote from a mom in one of the Facebook groups that I participate in, "I remember one day after a foster son's placement. He had been clingy, demanding, pushing me away, and starting fights. I opened the window and saw 3-inches of snow, and I realized school would be canceled. I promptly crawled back into bed and burst into tears." When I read her words, my heart resonated deeply with her sense of weariness and defeat. I have often felt like going back to bed, crawling deeply beneath my covers and staying there for days on end. It's not because I didn't care; I just didn't feel equipped to face the inevitable challenges, behaviors, and needs of the day. If you're reading this, chances are that's exactly what you're feeling right now.

You've put your heart and soul into classes, training, praying, and waiting for *this* child and the opportunity to help one who has been continually hurt and rejected. Yet here you are feeling hurt, rejected, and worn-out. Don't worry, you're not alone. I know it probably doesn't help to hear that this is normal. But it *is* normal, and it will pass. You *can* do this. You serve the same God that I do, and He is faithful to give you what you need to complete this mission and make a difference in the life of one of his most precious children.

> **"You've put your heart and soul into classes, training, praying and waiting for this child and the opportunity to help one who has been continually hurt and rejected."**

As we continue together over the next 29 days, we are going to journey through the very real emotions, questions, and pain of being a battle-weary parent. The struggle is very real, but we have a very real God who cares about you and will give you the wisdom, comfort, and understanding that you need to keep going. Be encouraged! You're not alone, you're not crazy, and you're not a failure. He will not let you stumble.

The only reasonable way to end this first day is to remind you that even King David, God's chosen one, found himself in the pits of despair needing the comfort of His God to help him make it through. I love his words in Psalm 121, "*I lift my eyes to the mountains – where does my help come from? My help comes from the Lord, the maker of heaven and earth. He will not let your foot slip – he who watches over you will not slumber; indeed, he who watches over Israel will neither slumber nor sleep. The Lord watches over you – the Lord is your shade at your right hand; the sun will not harm you by day nor the moon by night. The Lord will keep you from all harm – he will watch over your life; the Lord will watch over your coming and going both now and forevermore."*

Look up—your help comes from the Lord.

Scripture Meditation: Take a few moments to read the following Scriptures. Allow the Holy Spirit to speak to your heart about each of them.

Matthew 5:1-4 "One day as the crowds were gathering, Jesus went up the mountainside with his disciples and sat down to teach them. This is what he taught them, 'God blesses those who realize their need for him, for the Kingdom of Heaven is given to them. God blesses those who mourn for they will be comforted.'"

Psalm 31:9-10 "Have mercy on me, Lord, for I am in distress. My sight is blurred because of my tears. My body and soul are withering away. I am dying from grief; my years are shortened by sadness. Misery has drained my strength; I am wasting away from within."

John 14:27 "I am leaving you with a gift—peace of mind and heart. And the peace I give isn't like the peace the world gives. So don't be troubled or afraid."

Matthew 11:28-30 "Then Jesus said, 'Come to me, all of you who are weary and carry heavy burdens, and I will give you rest. Take my yoke upon you. Let me teach you, because I am humble and gentle, and you will find rest for your souls. For my yoke fits perfectly, and the burden I give you is light."

Capturing Thoughts: Throughout your adoption journey, I encourage you to capture your thoughts, fears, moments of joy, memories, and challenges. It will be a great encouragement to go back and read what you've written. Looking back, you'll be surprised how much you and your family grow throughout your experiences.

Prayer Starter: Father, we are tired. Our hearts are broken, and we feel like we've taken on much more than we can bear. We know you are faithful to hear our prayers and comfort us in the midst of our storm. Today, we're asking you for wisdom and understanding to continue this journey according to your will for our lives. Change our hearts, let us see through eyes of faith, renew our compassion, and reignite the passion for the fatherless that we had in the beginning.

Discussion Questions – Day 1: Your Help Comes From The Lord

1. What motivated you to get involved in foster care/adoption? As you reflect on your initial motivations, how do you feel about your current struggle?

2. Today's devotion says, "The struggle is very real, and we have a very real God who cares about you and will give you the wisdom, comfort, and understanding that you need to keep going." Talk about what this means for you and your family. What is it that you feel like you need to keep going?

3. Read Matthew 5:1-4. What do you think it means for you to mourn? How can this group help comfort you?

4. What are your biggest fears in this situation? Take time to put words to them—in writing, in conversation, or in prayer—so that they are exposed to the light and not hidden in darkness.

My Journey:

(Use this space to capture your thoughts, prayers, concerns and questions)

REMEMBER THE WORD TO YOUR SERVANT UPON WHICH YOU HAVE CAUSED ME
TO HOPE. THIS IS MY COMFORT IN MY AFFLICTION. FOR YOUR WORD HAS GIVEN
ME LIFE.

PSALMS 119:49

DAY 2: YOU CAN'T DO IT ALONE

It was Thanksgiving Day, but truthfully, there was little that I felt thankful for. Instead of enjoying a delicious meal with my family, I was driving alone on the interstate, angry at God, exhausted, and lacking what I thought was a proper heart-position to pray. In that moment, instead of my normal word-based and faith-filled prayers, I just spoke honestly with God. "I can't do this. You can't ask any more of me. I'm done." Then I cried. And then I cried a little more. In the deepest part of my soul, I felt broken, and I had absolutely nothing left. It was one of my most heartbreaking moments as a parent. A child that I so desperately loved was deeply lost in rebellion, bitterness, and anger; her behaviors were scary and completely out of my control. I felt alone, abandoned by God, and insecure in my own ability to handle the situation.

That day I learned that there are dark moments of the soul where the strength to put on a good face fades away, and all you're left with is raw, brutal emotion. It's in that moment, when the bottom completely falls out, that every prayer, every ounce of faith, and every quiet

"I had nothing new to give, nothing new to pray, and not a single scripture to hold onto. The only thing real to me was hurt, anger, worry and failure."

21

moment in scripture that I'd sown over time became a life raft that held me afloat. I had nothing new to give, nothing new to pray, and not a single scripture to hold onto. The only thing real to me was hurt, anger, worry, and failure.

I drove home numb. I crawled into my bed and called three specific friends and told each of them the whole truth about what was going on and asked them to pray on my behalf. In complete honesty, I said, "I don't have any prayers left. I have no words. All of the strength I have left in me is needed just to deal with tomorrow." Each of them said the same thing, "Go to bed. Rest. As a mom, pay attention to what only you as a mom can. I will cover you in prayer." As the days and weeks passed, these three precious friends covered our family in prayer. They shared scripture and promises with me daily that gave me hope and encouragement. God truly used them to provide our family with comfort in affliction, and on His word, we were able to hope.

As my strength returned, I was able to see God's mercy and care for me in the precious loyalty of my friends. This experience was a vivid reminder to me that we aren't called into this journey alone. If we allow ourselves to be vulnerable with trusted companions around us, God can use them to bring us strength and comfort in the midst of our sorrow. Going through crisis alone is a recipe for disaster, both for you and for your children.

When we're in crisis, we're vulnerable and weak. In those moments, it's easy to lose hope and feel like God has abandoned us. These moments require someone who can come alongside you to remind you of God's promises, His word, and the hope that you have in Him. Don't ever go through crisis alone. It will wreck you and take you out. Call trusted friends, and as my friend Chrissy says, "Tell them the truth. The good, the bad, and the disgustingly ugly truth." Give them the opportunity to encourage you, cover you, and help. God's word through caring friends will be your greatest comfort in affliction. You can't do it alone.

Scripture Meditation: Take a few moments to read the following Scriptures. Allow the Holy Spirit to speak to your heart about each of them.

Proverbs 19:20-21 "Get all the advice and instruction you can, so you will be wise the rest of your life. You can make many plans, but the Lord's purpose will prevail."

James 5:16 "Confess your sins to each other and pray for each other so that you may be healed. The earnest prayer of a righteous person has great power and produces wonderful results."

Romans 8:26-27 "And the Holy Spirit helps us in our weakness. For example, we don't know what God wants us to pray for. But the Holy Spirit prays for us with groanings that cannot be expressed in words. And the Father who knows all hearts knows what the Spirit is saying, for the Spirit pleads for us believers in harmony with God's own will."

Ecclesiastes 4:9-10 "Two people are better off than one, for they can help each other succeed. If one person falls, the other can reach out and help. But someone who falls alone is in real trouble."

Capturing Thoughts: Throughout your adoption journey, I encourage you to capture your thoughts, fears, moments of joy, memories, and challenges. It will be a great encouragement to go back and read what you've written before. Looking back, you'll be surprised how much you and your family grow through your experiences.

Prayer Starter: Father, I feel so alone. Grant me the wisdom to find trusted friends and advisors in this season. Give me the discernment to share our struggles, fears, and failures with someone who will lead me to your Word and pray truth and wisdom for me. I know that even in this trouble, you have a plan and a purpose. Thank you for coming to our rescue, even though we might not see it yet.

Discussion Questions – Day 2: You Can't Do It Alone

1. Have you ever reached a place where, as Pam describes, you have no prayers or words left? How did you get through it? How did it change your relationship with God?

2. Read Romans 8:26-27. The Holy Spirit clearly makes allowance for us in times when we're too weak to even know how to ask God for what we need. Why is it a challenge to trust His presence in these moments?

3. How does the idea that He is present with you and understands your weariness change the way you view God's provision in your struggle?

4. What is one thing you can do this week to invite someone else to join you in prayer and support? Write down three specific people that you want to trust with the truth—the good, the bad, and the disgustingly ugly truth.

My Journey:

(Use this space to capture your thoughts, prayers, concerns and questions)

Oh, Lord, I have so many enemies; so many are against me. So many are saying, 'God will never rescue him!' But you, O Lord, are a shield around me, my glory, and the one who lifts my head high. I cried out to the Lord, and he answered me from his holy mountain. I lay down and slept. I woke up in safety, for the Lord was watching over me. I am not afraid of ten thousand enemies who surround me on every side.

Psalms 3:1-6

DAY 3: HE IS SUSTAINING YOU

There have been so many times that I've been right there with David in this passage of scripture. Facing so many trials at once and having no one around who truly understood the depths of my despair or the fierceness of my hope that we would ultimately prevail. In this place when I felt so alone, I turned to the Lord, knowing that even in this, He was present, protecting, and providing. In great tears and choking agony, I cried out to Him and laid it all at His feet. I slept and awoke the next morning with a new strength to face the situation again for another day. Sometimes the situation had changed, but most of the time it hadn't. Nothing was different in the natural, what was different was inside me in the spiritual. I deeply trust God and His word—deeply. It was the only thing that could sustain me. period.

When you are in the midst of a conflict with your child. Or as we've been, in a crushing and tiring season of rebellion, rejection, and angst, the only hope you have to survive is your ability to see the Lord in the midst of the battle. In this passage of scripture, David clearly captures. three critical

26

components to surviving these tumultuous seasons.

First, you have to be honest about what's happening. David didn't start this prayer with, "Thank you, Lord, for another day. Although things look bad right now, I trust you." No. He started with, "This SUCKS! Everything around me is going wrong and everyone around me is clueless how to help and think I've completely lost my mind....and my salvation!" We have a tendency to sugar coat bad stuff because we feel like it lessens our witness. Simply put, that's a lie. God needs us to be real and raw with Him. And others need to see us turn to God and trust Him, even when it's bad, really bad. That's the only way they're going to know to turn to Him when their stuff is bad, too. It heightens our witness!

Second, you have to recognize that God alone is more than enough. Period. Although you're feeling overwhelmed and pressured, He is still your shield, and you have absolutely no idea how many other fiery darts of the enemy He is protecting you from at that very moment. No matter how bad things get, they could always be worse. I love the image that David paints here of the Lord being the lifter of our head. It brings to mind the image of a parent gently tilting a crying child's chin so that the child's eyes can meet theirs, and they can say, "It's all okay, honey." In the midst of our agony, He gently coaxes us to lift our tear-filled faces toward His, and hear His voice, "It's all going to be okay, honey." He alone is more than enough.

"In the midst of our agony, He gently coaxes us to lift our tear-filled faces toward His, and hear His voice, 'It's all going to be okay, honey.' He alone is more than enough.

Lastly, you have to allow yourself to rest. Your body, mind, and spirit all need the quiet of rest. Sleep is one of our body's most healing functions. Our minds sort out the issues from the day, making sense of sorrow and loss. Without sleep, we can't properly process thoughts and understanding. Have you ever gone to sleep thinking about a problem only to wake up the next morning and suddenly think of a solution? That isn't an accident. That's how He designed us. We need daily rest. In crisis, we need more rest. Don't allow the enemy to tell you it's selfish to nap and sleep. It's not, it's the best thing you can do to help solve the issue and gain the personal strength to keep going.

Like, David, we *will* find ourselves in moments where it feels like everything is falling apart and no one understands. But you are not alone. Don't fear the trial that sits before you. Trust in the God who knows all things, created all things, and promises that all things will work together for your good. He is sustaining you.

Scripture Meditation: Take a few moments to read the following Scriptures. Allow the Holy Spirit to speak to your heart about each of them.

Zephaniah 3:17 "For the Lord your God is living among you. He is a mighty savior. He will take delight in you with gladness. With his love, he will calm your fears. He will rejoice over you with joyful songs."

2 Corinthians 1:3-7 "All praise to God, the Father of our Lord Jesus Christ. God is our merciful Father and the source of all comfort. He comforts us in our troubles so that we can comfort others. When they are troubled, we will be able to give them the same comfort God has given us. For the more we suffer for Christ, the more God will shower us with his comfort through Christ. Even when we are weighed down with troubles, it is for your comfort and salvation! For when we ourselves are comforted, we will certainly comfort you. Then you can patiently endure the same things we suffer. We are confident that as you share in our sufferings, you will also share in the comfort God gives us."

Isaiah 43:2 "When you go through deep waters, I will be with you. When you go through rivers of difficulty, you will not drown. When you walk through the fire of oppression, you will not be burned up; the flames will not consume you."

Psalms 34:19 "The righteous person faces many troubles, but the Lord comes to the rescue each time."

Capturing Thoughts: Throughout your adoption journey, I encourage you to capture your thoughts, fears, moments of joy, memories, and challenges. It will be a great encouragement to go back and read what you've written before. Looking back, you'll be surprised how much you and your family grow through your experiences.

Prayer Starter: Lord, I have to be honest about how I feel right now. Everything about this situation is difficult. As I pour out my feelings, my anger, and my hurt to you, I trust that you know the absolute depths of my heart. I know that you are more than enough, and you can give me the patience and strength to weather this storm.

Discussion Questions – Day 3: He Is Sustaining You

1. Have you ever been truly honest in prayer and told God how you *really* feel about life? Why do you think it's so difficult to be brutally honest with God, even though we know he already knows?

2. Today's devotion says, "You have to recognize that God alone is more than enough." Is it easy for you to accept that all you need is God? Why do you think this recognition is important for you during this struggle?

3. Read Psalm 34:19. Why do you think the scripture isolates a "righteous person" when it talks about going through many trials?

4. How well are you currently resting? What is one thing you can do to make sure that you're getting the rest that you need to recover and build your strength?

My Journey:

(Use this space to capture your thoughts, prayers, concerns and questions)

THEN HE (JESUS) SAID TO THE MAN, 'STRETCH OUT YOUR HAND.'

SO HE STRETCHED IT OUT AND IT WAS COMPLETELY RESTORED, JUST

AS SOUND AS THE OTHER. BUT THE PHARISEES WENT OUT AND PLOTTED

HOW THEY MIGHT KILL JESUS.

MATTHEW 12:13 & 14

DAY 4: STRETCH OUT YOUR HAND

The most difficult place to be as a parent is in a position of opposition with a child that you deeply love. There's no end to the internal questioning, regret, and worry. What if I had done this? If only I had done that… it can seem unending. What's even worse is when others around you, and even your child, join in the battle of condemnation and accusation. Everyone has an opinion about why the current situation exists, what can be done to fix it, and where the fault lies. Instead of being in a position of strength to help our child, we find ourselves protecting and defending ourselves as parents.

For most parents, we've done the absolute best we could every step of the way and are the first ones to recognize when and where we could have done a better job. In order to help ourselves and our child, the first thing we have to do is recognize the battle is not ours; it's the Lord's. We must rely on His strength and walk in His peace in the midst of the storm. Even Jesus, perfect and in the act of bringing physical healing to broken bodies, was not spared accusation and condemnation! In the midst of doing the perfect work of healing, the Pharisees called

> **"In order to help ourselves and our child, the first thing we have to do is recognize the battle is not ours; it's the Lord's."**

a meeting and plotted to kill Him.

The context of this scripture is that Jesus was healing on the Sabbath, which was forbidden in the Pharisaical interpretation of God's law regarding keeping the Sabbath Day holy. The problem is that rather than the freedom and rest intended by God in this law, the Pharisees had corrupted the day into a one of self-denial and restriction. They were so caught up in their own enforced bondage that they failed to recognize the Healer of their mind, bodies, and souls was in their midst. Rather than accept freedom, hope, and healing, they lashed out in accusation, offense, and malice. He had broken their law, upset their apple cart, and he had to pay.

In the same way, we must recognize the Healer in our midst. He will restore your mind, body and soul and that of your child. However, we live in a world that must always find someone to blame. We blame ourselves, we accuse one another, we excuse our own behaviors because of what someone else has done, and the list goes on an on. Never forget that the kingdom of this world is not the Kingdom of our God & King, and the enemy who has been given temporary dominion is a deceiver and the accuser of the brethren. Anytime you are struggling with accusations being thrown at you or find yourself throwing them at others, you are functioning outside of partnership with God and aligning yourself with forces of darkness. Your job, in this process of restoration, is to free yourself from condemnation, from both yourself and others. And if you're struggling with accusation, offense, and malice toward your child, you must also let that go. A heart positioned for healing is a heart open and free from bitterness, offense, and judgment.

Doing our best, even when doing it in the name of Jesus, doesn't absolve us from the attacks of the enemy. It didn't for Jesus, so why should we assume we're any different? There's no question that parenting is a good work. God has entrusted us to steward and care for His most prized possessions, and we take our role seriously. This makes crisis and trial especially hard because you want to scream, "But I'm just trying to do a good thing!!!!!!" In reality, though, we're just the steward of their lives, we are not the author or creator of them. God loves them with an everlasting love; they are His creation, made in His image and according to His good purposes. Our role is to steward our children's hearts in partnership with Him, apart from our own opinions or those of others.

Oh, dear parent, don't withhold healing love, mercy, and kindness from yourself or your child. In the midst of trial, *stretch out your hand* to receive the healing mercy of God for your weary and worn soul. Then, you will be prepared to *stretch out your hand* to your child and offer restoration with a heart positioned in partnership with Jesus.

Scripture Meditation: Take a few moments to read the following Scriptures. Allow the Holy Spirit to speak to your heart about each of them.

Psalms 30:2-3 "O Lord my God, I cried out to you for help, and you restored my health. You brought me up from the grave, O Lord. You kept me from falling into the pit of death."

Psalms 118:16-17 "The strong right arm of the Lord is raised in triumph. The strong right arm of the Lord has done glorious things! I will not die, but I will live to tell what the Lord has done."

Isaiah 58:7-9 "I want you to share your food with the hungry and to welcome poor wanderers into your homes. Give clothes to those who need them, and do not hide from relatives who need your help. If you do these things, your salvation will come like the dawn. Yes, your healing will come quickly. Your godliness will lead you forward, and the glory of the Lord will protect you from behind. Then when you call, the Lord will answer, 'Yes, I am here,' he will quickly reply."

James 5:10-11 "For examples of patience in suffering, dear brothers and sisters, look at the prophets who spoke in the name of the Lord. We give great honor to those who endure under suffering. Job is an example of a man who endured patiently. From his experience we see how the Lord's plan finally ended in good, for he is full of tenderness and mercy."

Capturing Thoughts: Throughout your adoption journey, I encourage you to capture your thoughts, fears, moments of joy, memories, and challenges. It will be a great encouragement to go back and read what you've written before. Looking back, you'll be surprised how much you and your family grow through your experiences.

Prayer Starter: Lord, we feel like we're doing our best right now as stewards of our child's heart. We take this calling seriously, and our desire is to honor you and ultimately bring glory to your name through our story as a family. Your word promises us wisdom, it assures us that you are here in the midst of our suffering, and promises restoration for each of us. We're stretching out our hands right now so that you can mend and heal our wounded hearts. We trust your plan is full of tenderness and mercy, and as we seek to honor your Word, you will direct our steps.

Discussion Questions – Day 4: Stretch Out Your Hand

1. Today's devotion challenges us to stop the blame game—against us and against others. How much blame is going around in your current situation? What does it mean that the enemy is the accuser of the brethren? What steps can you take to shut down the voice of accusation in your home and heart?

2. Read Isaiah 58:7-9. Discuss how doing good for others leads to our own healing. Have you ever considered that part of your healing is a revealing of the ability of our own heart for sin (bitterness, anger, resentment, etc..)?

3. Talk about the relationship between "doing a good thing" as a parent and the challenges of dealing with difficult behaviors, rejection, defiance, and rebellion. How does the contradiction of those things contribute to your current struggle? Can you find a way to reconcile them in God's Word?

4. What areas of your own heart do you need to work on and ask God to heal? How will your ability to overcome those help you in your current situation with your child?

My Journey:

(Use this space to capture your thoughts, prayers, concerns and questions)

WHEN AN EVIL SPIRIT COMES OUT OF A MAN, IT GOES THROUGH ARID PLACES SEEKING REST AND DOES NOT FIND IT. THEN IT SAYS, 'I WILL RETURN TO THE HOUSE I LEFT.' WHEN IT ARRIVES, IT FINDS THE HOUSE UNOCCUPIED, SWEPT CLEAN AND PUT IN ORDER. THEN IT GOES AND TAKES WITH IT SEVEN OTHER SPIRITS MORE WICKET THAN ITSELF AND THEY GO IN AND LIVE THERE. AND THE FINAL CONDITION OF THAT MAN IS WORSE THAN THE FIRST.

MATTHEW 12:43-45

DAY 5: OUT OF BONDAGE

My friend Lesli and I often talk about the psychological profile of a foster or adoptive parent. They're strong, independent, self-sufficient, and proactive, traits that are certainly beneficial to them as they take on the role of parenting children from hard places. However, this make up of their strengths is also their greatest weakness. I should know…it's mine. The very parts of my personality that give me the grit to get into the messy places with my children are the very parts of my personality that set me up for major failure, isolation, and fatigue.

In this portion of scripture, Jesus is warning us about the bondage of thinking we're free from something in our life only to have it come back on us, only much worse, when our guard is down. Honestly, I see this happen a lot with battle-weary parents who are fighting for their children. They fight so long and so hard for and with their children that they totally lose sight of themselves and their own trauma, triggers, and tiredness. This is exactly the moment that the enemy returns and fills us with rage, disappointment, exhaustion, fear, worry, frustration, and resentment—seven wicked struggles that leave us in a terrible condition. It's a subtle process that totally takes us out of the game, if we let it.

Rejection, rebellion, and extreme behaviors hurt. It doesn't matter how ready you are to handle it. When it comes into your life and you find yourself in a position of crisis with your child, it hurts. Period. After you've given it your best and nothing seems to be working, you can find yourself withdrawing and becoming emotionally detached. Parenting children from hard places or crisis is a marathon, not a sprint. It's going to take a long time to cross the finish line and there will be many points along the way that your mental struggle will take you out long before physical ability does. In moments of exhaustion, it's tempting to give up and become apathetic and hopeless.

The only way to prevent this burnout and boomerang attack in your own life is to truly take care of yourself, body, mind, and spirit. Apathy is our enemy. We can *never* stop caring for others or for ourselves. In caring for ourselves we should understand our own triggers and become aware of our negative reactions to specific events in our family. Does a child's tone of voice cause you to shut down and withdraw or go on the offense and raise your voice? Can a particular look cause you to become irrationally angry because it reminds you of how someone else in your life treated you? Did you grow up as a child of parents who were abusive, absent, or ill-prepared for parenting? If so, when you're doing your best to *not* be like your parents, does it deeply hurt you when your child says they wish they had different parents or that they think you don't care? Dealing with the residual pain of our own loss, grief, and fear is critical to parenting in crisis. Take care of yourself and seek out safe places that you can unload your burden and sadness. It's only through your own vulnerability you can be fully available

> **"Be realistic with yourself. It's okay to grieve. It's okay to experience anger. It's okay to be hurt. You aren't super human, and no one expects you to be."**

to help your child heal through their crisis.

We must stay alert to the open doors in our lives that sidetrack us on the road to healing both for our children and ourselves. Keeping ourselves healthy along the way is the best way to keep those doors into our lives closed and remain on alert for the tactics and schemes of the enemy.

Be realistic with yourself. It's okay to grieve. It's okay to experience anger. It's okay to be hurt. You aren't super human, and no one expects you to be. Take time to refill your own tank. Do something today that you enjoy—read a book, pray, go on a walk, talk with a close friend, or simply lie in bed and watch your favorite show. Freedom is the way out of bondage. Give yourself the freedom to care for you. Your child needs it.

Scripture Meditation: Take a few moments to read the following Scriptures. Allow the Holy Spirit to speak to your heart about each of them.

> **Proverbs 15:1-4a** "A gentle answer turns away wrath, but harsh words stir up anger. The wise person makes learning a joy; fools spout only foolishness. The Lord is watching everywhere, keeping his eye on both the evil and the good. Gentle words bring life and health…"

> **Luke 6:27-31** "But if you are willing to listen, I say, love your enemies. Do good to those who hate you. Pray for the happiness of those who curse you. Pray for those who hurt you. If someone slaps you on one cheek, turn the other cheek. If someone demands your coat, offer your shirt also. Give what you have to anyone who asks you for it; and

when things are taken away from you, don't try to get them back. Do for others as you would like them to do for you."

Ephesians 4:26, 27, 29, 31 & 32 "And don't sin by letting anger gain control over you. Don't let the sun go down while you are still angry, for anger gives a mighty foothold to the devil. Don't use foul or abusive language. Let everything you say be good and helpful, so that your words will be an encouragement to those who hear them. Get rid of all bitterness, rage, anger, harsh words and slander, as well as all types of malicious behavior. Instead be kind to each other, tenderhearted, forgiving one another; just as God through Christ has forgiven you."

James 1:19-20 "My dear brothers and sisters, be quick to listen, slow to speak, and slow to get angry. Your anger can never make things right in God's sight."

Capturing Thoughts: Throughout your adoption journey, I encourage you to capture your thoughts, fears, moments of joy, memories, and challenges. It will be a great encouragement to go back and read what you've written before. Looking back, you'll be surprised how much you and your family grow through your experiences.

Prayer Starter: Jesus, we're hurt and angry. It's difficult to let it all go. We know that your Word tells us to not let anger gain control over us, but we're struggling. Give us the strength to listen, speak love and put aside anger so that we can love this child that you've given us to steward. Show us how to walk in compassion while being responsible to teach our child how to live a whole and righteous life.

Discussion Questions – Day 5: Out of Bondage

1. What negative emotions are you struggling with in this situation? Are you having difficulty letting them go?

2. Take time to evaluate the triggers and trauma in your own life. It's possible that you have buttons you're not aware of that are being pushed. Have you considered professional or spiritual counseling for your own past hurts?

3. Proverbs 15:1 talks about a soft answer turning away wrath. What are ways that your own battle-weariness has caused you to be harsh? Have you provoked anger in your child unintentionally through your own responses?

4. If everything we say should be good and helpful in order to be an encouragement to those who hear them, what's one way you can change how you speak to your child—especially in the midst of conflict? What effect do you think it could have on the outcome of your conflicts and arguments?

My Journey:

(Use this space to capture your thoughts, prayers, concerns and questions)

ALL PRAISE TO GOD, THE FATHER OF OUR LORD JESUS CHRIST. GOD IS OUR

MERCIFUL FATHER AND THE SOURCE OF ALL COMFORT. HE COMFORTS US IN

OUR TROUBLES SO THAT WE CAN COMFORT OTHERS. WHEN THEY ARE

TROUBLED, WE WILL BE ABLE TO GIVE THEM THE SAME COMFORT GOD HAS

GIVEN US. FOR THE MORE WE SUFFER FOR CHRIST, THE MORE GOD WILL

SHOWER US WITH HIS COMFORT THROUGH CHRIST. EVEN WHEN WE ARE

WEIGHED DOWN WITH TROUBLES, IT IS FOR YOUR COMFORT AND SALVATION!

FOR WHEN WE OURSELVES ARE COMFORTED, WE WILL CERTAINLY COMFORT

YOU. THEN YOU CAN PATIENTLY ENDURE THE SAME THINGS WE SUFFER. WE

ARE CONFIDENT THAT AS YOU SHARE IN OUR SUFFERINGS, YOU WILL ALSO

SHARE IN THE COMFORT GOD GIVES US.

2 CORINTHIANS 1:3-7

DAY 6: IT IS ABOUT YOU

I woke up this morning still in the midst of tribulation with one of our daughters. The struggles she's facing are so real, scary and heartbreaking that it feels nearly impossible to overcome them. I sat at my desk with my Bible open, looking. I was looking to build up my own faith, looking for answers for her, and desperately looking for something from God to take away the feelings of fear and uncertainty both of us are experiencing. First, I focused on building up my understanding of love. Then, I moved on to scriptures on innate worth. Finally, I tried to study trial and tribulation. As I dug through the Word for answers, lots of things were comforting, but nothing was the "it" that I felt like I should find. After a while, honestly, I was frustrated.

Finally, I stopped looking, closed my eyes and envisioned myself walking with Jesus and telling Him that I'm frustrated with the situation and anxious because I can't seem to find the answers. In that quiet moment with my eyes closed, I had a conversation with Him—not about what's written in the Bible but about what was hurting in my heart. Jesus softly and gently moved me from a focus on finding the answer to a place of being open and vulnerable about my feelings. My *feelings*. You see, I'm not a *feeling* girl. I'm a facts and faith girl. I *have* feelings but I don't *like* feelings, and I certainly don't often talk about them to other people. It's both a great strength and a crippling weakness for me. For Jesus to ask me to talk honestly about my feelings felt like ultimate weakness to me. What good are feelings? It's faith that's going to move this mountain. Let's focus on the one that needs help—my daughter—not me. So, I opened my eyes and picked up a different Bible and decided to keep looking for the answer. The problem all morning has obviously been that I'm reading the wrong version. After flipping through a few Psalms, I closed the Bible in frustration. Finally, I decided to quit running. Sometimes I'm just a little stubborn.

As I pulled out my notebook and picked up a pen I was certain this was a total waste of time. Okay, Jesus. You want to talk about my feelings? Fine. Here's what I wrote,

"I'm scared that the worst will happen. I'm unsure that things are going to get better and the uncertainty is causing me to feel anxious and worried. I don't like those feelings. I feel alone, like I don't really have anyone to talk to who can understand. I'm overwhelmed because it feels like more than I can bear. Honestly, I'm angry. This isn't fair for all of us. It's not fair that she's suffering and in pain. Focusing on how I feel is making me feel selfish because this isn't about me and focusing on me feels like a waste of time. That's frustrating to me. I am really hopeful because I do believe that God's word is true, but I'm discouraged because nothing seems to be working or helping. I'm fearful that I'm going to say or do the wrong thing and cause more hurt and pain."

I put down the pen and paper and stared at the words on the page. God spoke softly to my heart and said, "There's a big difference between how you feel and what you know. By ignoring your feelings and focusing only on the facts/faith you are short circuiting the healing that I need to do in your heart as you go through this trial." Ok, I get it. Now that we've gone through this little exercise, can we go back to some answers?

You're probably much smarter than I and have already figured out that Jesus wasn't done. The next thing He prompted me to do was to text my daughter and vulnerably tell her that I'm struggling too. WHAT?!?!?! She is going through enough on her own without me adding in my *feelings* too! I'm her MOTHER. I'm supposed to be the strong one who builds up her faith and speaks life into the situation. I can't crumble now. I just can't. I blankly stared at my phone for a long time. A very long time.

Finally, I typed out everything that I had written on paper into a text and told her that I needed to be vulnerable with her. She responded almost immediately and her response brought me to my knees in a puddle of tears—the ugly cry kind. Here are a few snippets of her message to me, "Your honesty and vulnerability… it's an honor to hear you say those things. I want us to grow closer during this time, even though it's messy. Don't feel alone, don't feel discouraged, don't get frustrated. Trust Jesus and know that you and dad are going above and beyond, even though it may not feel like it. We WILL come out of this triumphant and victorious because He loves us. Because He died for this, for us. He's for us, not against us. And when He's for us, no attack of the enemy can succeed." I'd searched all morning for a scripture to calm my fears, but no greater comfort could be found than to lay my heart open before both my Jesus and my hurting daughter and have her return to me with the Word of God and her own confession of faith.

To say this is a breakthrough for me is an understatement. You see, I didn't feel like I was the one that needed healing. I have been asking for healing for my daughter, for all of my daughters, on a daily basis. *I'm* fine. *I've* got this. But truly, I don't and, to be totally honest, my pretending that I do is doing more harm than good for my entire family and me. I confessed and repented because I had it totally wrong. This life of Christ, this life of parenting, this thing we call family—it IS about me. It's about me allowing those I love to comfort me. It's about me getting in the mess and *sharing in the sufferings*—not solving them, *feeling* them. Weeping. Fearing. Feeling. If I'm truly following Christ's example and the example of Paul in today's scripture, I'm in the mess and am therefore also messy—unashamedly and without having any answer aside from Jesus.

> **"If I'm following Christ's example and the example of Paul in today's scripture, I'm in the mess and am therefore also messy—unashamedly and without having any answer aside from Jesus."**

Scripture Meditation: Take a few moments to read the following Scriptures. Allow the Holy Spirit to speak to your heart about each of them.

I realize this isn't a scripture, but it's a great quote from C.S.

47

Lewis on the topic of vulnerability that fits well into the meditations for today. "Love anything and your heart will be wrung and possibly broken. If you want to make sure of keeping it intact, you must give it to no one, not even an animal. Wrap it carefully round with hobbies and little luxuries; avoid all entanglements. Lock it up safe in a casket or coffin of your selfishness. But in that casket, safe, dark, motionless, airless, it will change. It will not be broken; it will become unbreakable, impenetrable, irredeemable. To love is to be vulnerable."

2 Corinthians 12:8-10 "Three different times I begged the Lord to take it away. Each time he said, 'My gracious favor is all you need. My power works best in your weakness.' So now I am glad to boast about my weaknesses, so that the power of Christ may work through me. Since I know it is all for Christ's good, I'm quite content with my weaknesses and with insults, hardships, persecutions, and calamities. For when I am weak, then I am strong."

Psalms 69:13-14 "But I keep right on praying to you, Lord, hoping this time you will show me favor. In your unfailing love, O God, answer my prayer with your sure salvation. Pull me out of the mud; don't let me sink any deeper! Rescue me from those who hate me and pull me from these deep waters."

2 Corinthians 4:7-10 "But this precious treasure—this light and power that now sine within us—is held in perishable containers, that is, in our weak bodies. So everyone can see that our glorious power is from God and is not our own. We are pressed on every side by troubles, but we are not crushed and broken. We are perplexed, but we don't give up and quit. We are hunted down, but God never abandons us. We get knocked down but we get up again and keep going. Through suffering, these bodies of ours constantly share in the death of Jesus so that the life of Jesus may also be seen in our bodies."

Capturing Thoughts: Throughout your adoption journey, I encourage you to capture your thoughts, fears, moments of joy, memories, and challenges. It will be a great encouragement to go back and read what you've written before. Looking back, you'll be surprised how much you and your family grow through your experiences.

Prayer Starter: God, there are so many things that I have hidden deep inside. I'm afraid to share how I truly feel, with you or with any one else. I know that my thoughts are sometimes based in fear, often built on anger and mixed up in doubt and confusion. Yet, your Word calls me to be like David and pour out my innermost fears. I know that it's in my weakness that you're made strong. Help me in my weakness to not be prideful. Give me the strength, Lord, to be weak and needy.

Discussion Questions – Day 6: It IS About You

1. What does vulnerability mean to you? Do you find it easy or difficult to admit your weaknesses and fears?

2. Read 2 Corinthians 4:7-10. Talk about why your weakness allows God's glorious power to shine? What does it mean for you to "get knocked down, but get up again and keep going?"

3. Talk about Pam's interaction with her daughter. How do you feel about her vulnerability? How do you feel about her daughter's response?

4. Are there things that you can say to your child that might help them to

gain a new perspective on family and relationships that also requires you to be vulnerable? Share your plan with the group and allow them to give you honest feedback on your motive and tone. Be careful to not be vengeful in a "see how you make me feel" way.

My Journey:

(Use this space to capture your thoughts, prayers, concerns and questions)

DAY 7: MOVED WITH COMPASSION

I recently traveled back to my hometown in Kentucky to attend the funeral of my Uncle who had passed away suddenly. I spent the majority of my time with my Dad at the funeral home, visiting with friends and family whom I hadn't seen in twenty-plus years. Most were curious to hear what I had done in life and were surprised to learn that I had seven daughters, six adopted. Responses to our family's story ranged from, "Wow! You're doing such an awesome thing!" to "There's no way I could do that!" and the inevitable, "But don't they have a lot of issues?" After telling and retelling our story over a two-day period, I developed a pretty good set of standard answers to questions which allowed me to dispel the curiosity, show off a few photos, and move on to another topic quickly. Then, one conversation changed it all.

Although I was hundreds of miles away from home, there were still some pretty significant things going on. Things were happening I didn't understand, and honestly, I was grateful to be away for a few days, even if for a funeral. Talking about my family to others who were amazed and encouraging enabled me to focus my thoughts and words on the beauty of our story and forget the mess, if only for a moment. In a very human way, I was convincing myself that things were just as good in reality as my stories made them seem. In truth, things at home were messy and tiring. Five of our seven were back under our roof with 100% of them struggling through major life decisions, transition, and coping with issues of trauma resurfacing in the face of their own uncertainty. I found myself distancing myself from the issues because I didn't have answers and was overwhelmed with my own stuff. I knew what I was doing and told myself that after all I'd been through, I deserved a little mental and emotional break. I'm sure I did, but Jesus was about to call me back out of my self-imposed break and remind me of the work He's prepared me for all of my life.

After the funeral, the little Baptist church that I had grown up in catered a late lunch for our family and friends. It was surreal for me to be there again, with people that I'd known as a child, in a place that had been central to so much of my childhood. The church's choir director from my childhood approached me and said, "Pam, I was lying in bed last night thinking about you and what you've done with your family. It's incredible. Can I ask you a personal question?" I said, "Of course." He asked, "Why do you do it? Adopt and care for these kids?" Well, that's easy, I thought. I gave him my most amazing spiritual answer, "Because the Bible says to… in James 1:27 it says that pure religion is caring for widows and orphans….in Psalm 68:5 & 6 it says that God sets the lonely in family….how could I *not* answer the call of Jesus to care for the fatherless?" Boom! Nailed it, scripture and all. The look on his face and the shaking of his head to indicate "no" told me otherwise. He said, "Let me ask it a different way, do you think the way you grew up has anything to do with it?" In an instant the Holy Spirit used his simple question to totally shake me to the core. To be clear, I'm not oblivious to the fact that my childhood has had a huge bearing on why I do what I do in our family. I've shared that many times. But this was different. Other people that I share it with, they don't *know*. This man, he *knew*. This statement from a man who had watched me grow up and has known me *all of my life* shook me.

Staring into his face, I saw the truth of what the Lord was using him to remind me of—my own brokenness. In this conversation, I couldn't gloss over the truth of my childhood and the struggles of our family. The absolute miracle it is that I'm leading the life

"It's incredibly easy on this journey to lose sight of compassion in the midst of the daily grind of family."

that I am, in spite of it all. He was staring into the face of a little girl who had all odds stacked against her, yet God had used it and redeemed it all. I couldn't deny the brokenness that surrounded me as a child, and as I reflected on all that he must know and remember, I was moved by the look of compassion on his face. Standing there in that hallway, Jesus showed me, again, what it felt like to have someone see all of your stuff, all of your pain, all of your brokenness, and patiently understand. It was a healing moment for me as he quietly acknowledged, with one simple question, that my pain and struggle were real. God saw them and so did he. As we conversed about the ways in which my childhood shaped me into becoming the mom that I am today, I sensed Jesus calling me back to the work that He had uniquely molded me for all of my life—to be moved with compassion for my children's brokenness and see their stuff, their pain, and their brokenness and patiently understand.

It's incredibly easy on this journey to lose sight of compassion in the midst of the daily grind of family. Quickly we can become so focused on the frustrating issues of school, behavior, routines, and correction that we forget the pain and loss that brought our children into our lives. And it's especially easy when you're battle-weary and in the very midst of crisis. In our children's most desperate and hurtful moments, we absolutely cannot afford to lose sight of the inner struggles and pain that they are battling. In nearly every instance that the Bible records Jesus as being "moved with compassion," healing follows. For our family and our children to experience healing, we must allow our hearts to continually be moved with compassion toward them. Where compassion leads, healing follows.

Scripture Meditation: Take a few moments to read the following Scriptures. Allow the Holy Spirit to speak to your heart about each of them.

Matthew 14:14 "A vast crowd was there as he stepped from the boat, and he had compassion on them and healed their sick."

Mark 6:34 "A vast crowd was there as he stepped from the boat, and he had compassion on them because they were like sheep without a shepherd. So he taught them many things."

Romans 12:20 "Instead, do what the Scriptures say: 'If your enemies are hungry, feed them. If they are thirsty, give them something to drink, and they will be ashamed of what they have done to you."

Colossians 3:12-13 "Since God chose you to be the holy people whom he loves, you must clothe yourselves with tenderhearted mercy, kindness, humility, gentleness, and patience. You must make allowance for each other's faults and forgive the person who offends you. Remember the Lord forgave you, so you must forgive others."

Capturing Thoughts: Throughout your adoption journey, I encourage you to capture your thoughts, fears, moments of joy, memories, and challenges. It will be a great encouragement to go back and read what you've written before. Looking back, you'll be surprised how much you and your family grow through your experiences.

Prayer Starter: Father, grant me a heart of compassion for the hurts, brokenness, and confusion that my child is experiencing. Allow me to be moved with compassion so that through my mercy, kindness, and patience, you can do the work of healing. I want to share the truth of your love through the example of my love for them. Show me ways that I can reach their heart in words and actions.

Discussion Questions – Day 7: Moved With Compassion

1. Have you ever experienced someone showing you compassion and mercy, even when you didn't deserve it? Explain how this made you feel.

2. Today's devotion says, "In nearly every instance that the Bible records Jesus as being 'moved with compassion,' healing follows. For our family and our children to experience healing, we must allow our hearts to continually be moved with compassion toward them. Where compassion leads, healing follows." In what ways does that challenge you? In what ways does it encourage you?

3. Talk about a time you were moved with compassion for your child. What happened?

4. What are some specific areas of healing that you're praying for in your child? How can this group support you and pray with you?

My Journey:

(Use this space to capture your thoughts, prayers, concerns and questions)

HE WILL NOT QUARREL OR CRY OUT; NO ONE WILL HEAR HIS VOICE IN THE
STREETS. A BRUISED REED HE WILL NOT BREAK, AND A SMOLDERING WICK HE
WILL NOT SNUFF OUT, 'TIL HE HAS BROUGHT JUSTICE THROUGH TO VICTORY.
MATTHEW 12: 19-20

DAY 8: THROUGH TO VICTORY

This word picture of Jesus is one of my absolute favorites. He came into
the world to redeem the world and the world rejected Him. Yet, even in the
midst of rejection, he did not quarrel or cry out, and He didn't go through
the streets proclaiming His defense. In my opinion, one of the most
accurate scripture pictures of our Savior is painted in the last sentence, "...*a
bruised reed he will not break, and a smoldering wick he will not snuff out, til he has
brought justice through to victory.*" A bruised reed is a piece of long grass that is
useful for making baskets, thatching roofs, and many other things. They
become bruised when they are walked through or trampled upon, as this
bends them and makes them weak and not useful. It was common to just
break them in half and throw them away. In the same way, a smoldering
wick doesn't absorb the oil well and causes the light to flicker instead of
shining consistently. It also puts off a thick black smoke that's annoying and
has to be washed off. Our Jesus is patient and kind, and He will not break
us when we're already bruised and trampled on; He won't give up on us
when we're struggling and

> "Our Jesus is patient and kind, and He will not break us when we're already bruised and trampled on; He won't give up on us when we're struggling and inconsistent."

inconsistent. Instead, He bears with us until He has brought justice and sees it through to victory!

Our children are bruised reeds and smoldering wicks. Life tramples all of us from time to time but for most of us, it didn't trample us before we had a voice and a choice. That's not the case for our children. We have to remember that this battle isn't personal. The words you're hearing and the actions you're witnessing probably feel very personal, but they aren't. Regardless of how long you've been in your foster or adopted child's life, I'm sure you've done the best you can every step of the way. You've made mistakes and hopefully taken time to repair those mistakes through repentance. We all have. But mistakes don't make you a failure, quitting does. We must not allow ourselves to get to a place of consistently defending ourselves, quarreling, and making our case. This takes us away from the hard work of healing, which requires we walk near our children.

In the same way that Jesus walked the earth through false accusation, persecution, plotting, and ultimately death on a cross while keeping His love and mission on our behalf in front Him, we as parents must continually remind ourselves of our love and mission on behalf of *our* children. In walking out this journey, we must give our bruised children an opportunity to heal. It's so easy to break the bruised spirit of a child, especially in the midst of crisis. In my own life, I've allowed my frustration to take over my mouth and common sense way too many times to count and as a result, deeply wounded my children. Chastising our children to "grow up," "have thicker skin," "not be so emotional," or "get over it" isn't helpful, especially in the heat of battle. We must choose our words carefully. Words can *truly* break you.

It takes time and patience to bear with a smoldering wick; it can be frustrating and messy. It takes the same time and patience to bear with our children who are struggling to absorb our love and reacting with messy behaviors and rejection. It's so natural to just want to snuff out the behavior and move on. Yet, the harder work of healing calls us to get into the mess with our children and help them dig beyond the behavior to the survival instincts and feelings that are its driving forces. There's no doubt that bedwetting, constant lying, running away, rages and a myriad of other common behaviors resulting from trauma are frustrating and tiring. We simply have to remind ourselves over and over that overcoming neglect, grief, loss, and abandonment is a lifetime journey, and it's our role as parents to be available—for life.

God's word isn't short on promises of healing, deliverance, and hope—in those things we can trust. He promises justice for our own hurts and for those of our children. As parents we must partner with Him until justice is brought and continually walk with our children *through to victory.*

Scripture Meditation: Take a few moments to read the following Scriptures. Allow the Holy Spirit to speak to your heart about each of them.

Proverbs 25:15 "Patience can persuade a prince, and soft speech can crush strong opposition."

Romans 15:4-5 "Such things were written in the Scriptures long ago to teach us. They give us hope and encouragement as we wait patiently for God's promises. May God, who gives this patience and encouragement, help you live in complete harmony with each other— each with the attitude of Christ Jesus toward the other."

Galatians 5:22-26 "But when the Holy Spirit controls our lives, he will produce this kind of fruit in us: love, joy, peace, patience, kindness, goodness, faithfulness, gentleness, and self-control. Here there is no conflict with the law. Those who belong to Christ Jesus have nailed the passions and desires of their sinful nature to his cross and crucified them there. If we are living now by the Holy Spirit, let us follow the Holy Spirit's leading in every part of our lives. Let us not become conceited, or irritate one another, or be jealous of one another."

1 Thessalonians 5:14-15 "Brothers and sisters, we urge you to warn those who are lazy. Encourage those who are timid. Take tender care of those who are weak. Be patient with everyone. See that no one pays back evil for evil, but always try to do good to each other and to everyone else."

Capturing Thoughts: Throughout your adoption journey, I encourage you to capture your thoughts, fears, moments of joy, memories, and challenges. It will be a great encouragement to go back and read what you've written before. Looking back, you'll be surprised how much you and your family grow through your experiences.

Prayer Starter: Lord, it's hard sometimes to bear with our child in difficult behaviors and defiance. Reveal to us any area that, in our words or actions, we could be bruising or breaking our child's spirit. Teach us how to operate in the fruits of the Spirit, even when we're frustrated, hurt, and exhausted. We trust your plans are better than ours, and you will uphold your promises to bring healing to our child.

Discussion Questions – Day 8: Through to Victory

1. What do you notice about how Jesus deals with the hurting and broken

in this devotion? How does this challenge you in your personal life and family?

2. Today's devotion says, "mistakes don't make you a failure, only quitting does." Have you felt like quitting? Talk about how this makes you feel.

3. Read 1 Thessalonians 5:14-15. This scripture reiterates the importance of balancing instruction and correction with patience. How well do you balance the two in your parenting?

4. Talk about a time that you chose patience and grace in response to your child's behavior. How did your child react to it?

My Journey:

(Use this space to capture your thoughts, prayers, concerns and questions)

Do not be afraid of them. Remember the Lord, great and awesome, and fight for your brethren, your sons, your daughters, your wives, and your houses.

NEHEMIAH 4:14

DAY 9: DO NOT BE AFRAID

Do not be afraid. That's much easier said than done. In crisis, it seems there is everything to be afraid of, and when you're battle-weary, those fears can be overwhelming. The truth is simple. We're in a battle for the hearts and minds of our children; we're in a battle for the health of our family. Family is the very thing God has called us to build in His name, and it is the very thing that the enemy wants to tear down and destroy. Never forget your role, parent. You are the guardians of the gate for your home, and make no mistake, this is war.

Nehemiah is a great example of the leadership required of a foster and adoptive parent. It's our job to lead the rebuilding and repairing of walls in our children's lives that were torn down long before we came along. In Nehemiah, we see a battle-*ready* leader who's leading his nation from a position of compassion, repentance, and unity. Nehemiah had a comfortable and safe life as the cupbearer of the king. Yet the minute he learned that the walls of Jerusalem were torn down and his beloved nation was exposed to attack, he was moved with compassion for them and wept for days. Out of his compassion God placed him in the position to lead the people of Israel in the rebuilding of their walls. At one time, we were all moved with compassion on behalf of our children's stories, and now, God has placed us in the position to lead them in the rebuilding of their lives.

Like Nehemiah, we must respond.

The rebuilding of the wall for Nehemiah began with a strong sense of unity and a clear purpose. The people responded to his leadership, and side-by-side, they began making progress. The wall was being rebuilt!

But then...isn't there always a "but then." But then the people began murmuring and complaining, outsiders began to say negative things, and those who were dedicated began to lose their steam. Sound familiar? "Things seemed like they were going great! But then...." "We've been getting along wonderfully. But then...." "He's been respectful and obedient. But then...." "Her grades have been improving and she's been enjoying school. But then..." *But then* is the critical juncture of leadership in business, war, and family alike. What you do after the *but then* shapes the outcome.

Be vigilant and be careful. But do not be afraid.

Apart from being sensitive to the Lord and placing all of his plans before Him for direction, there were three additional key decisions that Nehemiah made which resulted in his success in rebuilding the wall. As parents of children from hard places, we are rebuilders of walls and must also remain close to the Lord and make these same three decisions:

> **"We must allow our children to fight alongside us, and sometimes, carry the sword. Trust the Spirit of the Lord who is at work within them."**

First, teamwork is required. Everyone has a place, and we all must know our purpose. Nehemiah used *everyone* to rebuild the wall,, mothers, fathers, sons, and daughters. He kept the families together and kept purpose and hope in front of them at all times. As parents, we are the guardians of the gates, but we aren't the only builders of the wall. We must work diligently at modeling and creating an atmosphere of teamwork and unity within our families. We must also allow our children to fight alongside us, and sometimes, carry the sword. Trust the Spirit of the Lord who is at work within them. Allow them to see you as teachable and willing to listen to their opinions and ideas on wall building. Trust me, they'll probably surprise you.

Two, the right attitude must be combined with the right actions. When we take on the attitude that this is a marathon and not a sprint, it's easier to understand that we'll lose small battles along the way, but ultimately we will win the war, as long as we do not quit. Nehemiah modeled the right attitude among the people: *do not be afraid* but carry your weapon and stay together. In the same way, we, as a family, must not be afraid of the battles and attacks that come upon us, but we must be vigilant to arm ourselves and learn how to use our weapons. The builders on the wall repaired bricks with one hand and carried a sword with the other, always ready to defend themselves against attack. Be patient and be ready.

Three, we never let down our guard. I've been known to say, "It seems like every time we try to get away (my husband and I) to relax and rejuvenate, we come back, and it's ten times worse than when we left." That's my first clue that we left the wall exposed. No matter how good things seem to be going, we can never let down our guard. As parents and as entire family units, we must continually be on our guard against any force—internal or external—that would seek to divide us and tear down our walls.

I love the very next scripture, Nehemiah 4:15, "*And it happened, when our enemies heard that it was known to us, and that God had brought their plot to nothing, that all of us returned to the wall, everyone to his work.*" It is hard work to build family; everyone has his own responsibility in making it happen. Sometimes we build, and sometimes we turn and fight. As we lead our families in unity of purpose, the mind of Christ and on guard against the enemy, we will expose and repair the schemes of the enemy. Together, we'll do the work and the end result will be a lifetime legacy of faith and family. Do not be afraid.

Scripture Meditation: Take a few moments to read the following Scriptures. Allow the Holy Spirit to speak to your heart about each of them.

Ecclesiastes 4:9-12 "Two people can accomplish more than twice as much as one; they get a better return for their labor. If one person falls, the other can reach out and help. But people who are alone when they fall are in real trouble. And on a cold night, two under the same blanket can gain warmth from each other. But how can one be warm alone? A person standing alone can be attacked and defeated, but two can stand back-to-back and conquer. Three are even better, for a triple-braided cord is not easily broken."

1 Corinthians 12:12, 18, 22-26 "The human body has many parts, but the many parts make up only one body. So it is with the body of Christ. But God made our bodies with many parts, and he has put each part where he wants it. In fact, some of the parts that seem weakest and least important are really the most necessary. And the parts we regard as less honorable are those with clothe with the greatest care. So we carefully protect from the eyes of others those parts that should not be seen, while other parts do not require this special care. So God has put the body together in such a way that extra honor and care are given to those parts that have less dignity. This makes for harmony among the members, so that all the members care for each other equally. If one part suffers, all the parts suffer with it, and if one part is honored, all the parts are glad."

Galatians 3:28 "There is no longer Jew or Gentile, slave or free, male or female. For you are all Christians—you are one in Christ Jesus."

Philippians 2:3-5 "Don't be selfish; don't live to make a good impression on others. Be humble, thinking of others as better than yourself. Don't think only about your own affairs, but be interested in others, too, and what they are doing. Your attitude should be the same that Christ Jesus had."

Capturing Thoughts: Throughout your adoption journey, I encourage you to capture your thoughts, fears, moments of joy, memories, and challenges. It will be a great encouragement to go back and read what you've written before. Looking back, you'll be surprised how much you and your family grow through your experiences.

Prayer Starter: God, teach us how to lead our family as a team. As a family unit, we are called to glorify you through our unity. Grant us the wisdom to draw all members of our family together and create unity. Give us creative strategies to engage our children in meaningful ways as true participating members of the family, to help them feel ownership and usefulness.

Discussion Questions – Day 9: Do Not Be Afraid

1. In today's devotion, Pam talks about those "…but then" moments. What is the "but then" in your family's story? How can you go back and rebuild the wall that was torn down at that moment?

2. Read 1 Corinthians 12:12, 18, 22-26. If you think of your family members as each being different but equally important, what distinct gifts and abilities does each member bring? How can you honor those individual gifts and give them prominence in your household this week?

3. What does it mean to be teachable and willing to listen to your children? Do you practice this well at home? If so, talk to the group about your habits in this area. If not, talk to the group about your challenges in this area.

4. What walls are currently torn down in your family (trust, patience, affection, etc.)? Talk about how you can begin to rebuild them as a team. How can this group pray for you in the process?

My Journey:

(Use this space to capture your thoughts, prayers, concerns and questions)

WHILE HE WAS STILL SPEAKING, SOME CAME FROM THE RULER OF THE
SYNAGOGUE'S HOUSE WHO SAID, 'YOUR DAUGHTER IS DEAD. WHY TROUBLE
THE TEACHER ANY FURTHER?' AS SOON AS JESUS HEARD THE WORD THAT WAS
SPOKEN, HE SAID TO THE RULER OF THE SYNAGOGUE, 'DO NOT BE AFRAID,
ONLY BELIEVE."

MARK 5:35-36

DAY 10: WHY PUT UP WITH ALL OF THIS?

In this scripture, Jesus sets the example for shutting down the false report
and choosing to believe. We have to be vigilant against negative input into
our family story. There aren't many people who truly understand the
journey of a foster and adoptive family, so we have to be purposeful in
surrounding ourselves with people who do understand and will speak life
and hope into our circumstances. In crisis we need healing for the whole
family, and we must guard ourselves against division and doubt.

I've been in crisis many times in my journey as a mom of children from
hard places. I've also walked and talked with many families in crisis, and
every time, there is one common doubt and question we've all faced. It
often arrives in the form of a question from a "well-meaning" friend, "*Why
put up with all of this?*" In this one little question lay all of our doubts, all of
our insecurities, and all of our fears. It's the "Did I do the right thing?"
doubt. It's the, "Are we the right family?" wonder. It's the, "Things may
never change" fear. And it's the "Look what you're doing to your *own*
family" accusation.

It hurts. It's real. It's scary.

But it's a lie. Straight from the pits of darkness.

Let's be clear, *everyone* in the family is affected by this journey. As we step out to become parents and siblings of children from hard places, we all experience the side effects of trauma, grief, and loss. It's not easy to walk alongside someone that's hurting, especially when you love them deeply. You feel their pain, take the brunt of their anger, and often feel helpless or hopeless. Every member of the family

"As we step out to become parents and siblings of children from hard places, we all experience the side effects of trauma, grief, and loss. It's not easy to walk alongside someone that's hurting, especially when you love them deeply."

feels these things—father, mother, brother, and sister. Trauma hurts everyone, yet bearing with one another and sharing in suffering *is* the call of the cross. The truth in crisis is that we must care for ourselves, care for everyone in our family and trust the Lord with the outcomes.

We must not doubt or waver in God's calling upon our lives. However, standing firm in your calling doesn't mean that we become doormats allowing violence, rejection, rebellion, bad behaviors, or attitudes to run amuck in our home. It simply means that we stand firm in the call that God has called us into while making our home a safe place for everyone and leaning into Jesus for wisdom and discernment. Negativity and false reports calling into question the commitment that you've made aren't helpful. Seek real advice and counsel. There are plenty of options other than quitting and blaming ourselves.

God's Word is clear on promises. Our yes is to be yes and our no to be no.

Once you've promised forever to a child from a hard place, God expects you to honor your word as a representative of Him. Quitting, giving up, or giving the child "back" just simply isn't an option as a Christ follower. Having said that, please don't misinterpret my intention. I've walked with many families that could not allow a child to continue under their roof for a season because the child's needs demanded greater intervention than they could provide at home. Residential care, hospitalization, respite, alternate temporary living arrangements—these are all viable last resort options. You should never endanger yourself or anyone in your home by allowing a violent or abusive child to remain. Those in your home need your protection, and the child needs your help. You can do both without giving up and walking out of a child's life forever. Making the hard decision to seek alternative out-of-the-home care for a child tells everyone within the home that you care for them and are protecting them from further trauma and harm. Sticking by that child's side while in external placement arrangements and continuing visits, phone calls, and overnight stays tells that child that you love them, and you're still their family, no matter what.

We must acknowledge that fostering is different from adoption, but the principles of Christ remain the same. In fostering, your promise is different. You promise a temporary place of safety and love while the child's family is getting back on their feet. In emergency placements, there's little you can do to determine if a child's behaviors and history will create chaos or difficulty within your home. Be clear from the very beginning with every child that this is *temporary* because you are praying for their parents and family to be able to be back together, but that you love them *forever*, even after they go back home. Additionally, there are very real reasons to request that a child be moved to another home that's better suited to meet their needs. Your role is to love them through the transition and speak life and hope into them along the way. Prayerfully do all that you can to limit additional layers of rejection, abandonment, and loss in their lives.

Walking with your child in the midst of crisis will look differently for every family. There are tough decisions to be made in the process and gut wrenching actions to be taken. However, we can never find ourselves proclaiming to be a Christ-follower and abandoning a child that we've promised forever. Jesus gives the perfect example in response to the ultimate of fatalistic reports, *"as soon as Jesus heard the word that was spoken, He said, 'Do not be afraid, only believe.'"* The only final answer in any of our lives is Jesus, and His answer is hope. Always.

Scripture Meditation: Take a few moments to read the following Scriptures. Allow the Holy Spirit to speak to your heart about each of them.

Matthew 5:37 "Just say a simple, 'Yes, I will,' or 'No, I won't,' Your word is enough."

Matthew 13:58 "And so he only did a few miracles there because of their own unbelief."

Mark 9:24 "The father instantly replied, 'I do believe, but help my unbelief.'"

John 20:27 "Then he said to Thomas, 'Put your finger here and see my hands. Put your hand into the wound on my side. Don't be faithless any longer. Believe!'"

James 1:6 "But when you ask him, be sure that you really expect him to answer, for a doubtful mind is as unsettled as a wave of the sea that is driven and tossed by the wind."

Capturing Thoughts: Throughout your adoption journey, I encourage you to capture your thoughts, fears, moments of joy, memories, and challenges. It will be a great encouragement to go back and read what you've written before. Looking back, you'll be surprised how much you and your family grow through your experiences.

Prayer Starter: Jesus, I do believe that my family will be okay, and you called us to this journey, but help my unbelief. I'm struggling with insecurity and often don't feel like I'm up to the task that you've entrusted to me. I know that the only hope is found in you. Give me the ability to make the tough decisions, stick through the challenging times and never doubt the call that you've placed on my life, and on my family

Discussion Questions – Day 10: Why Put Up With All of This?

1. Think about a time that you made a decision that was right for your life, but many around you doubted you. How did you feel? What gave you the ability to go on?

2. Read Mark 9:14-29. In the story of this little boy, the father was exhausting every resource he had to find him help and he knew that only Jesus could make the difference. How does his honest expression of faith and doubt in verse 24 resonate with you?

3. In today's devotion Pam talks about never finding yourself in a position where you're proclaiming to be a Christ-follower and then abandoning or breaking promises to a child that you've committed to help. How does this challenge you?

4. Have you ever had someone give up on you? How did it feel? If you're feeling like quitting, how can this group be a better support to you?

My Journey:

(Use this space to capture your thoughts, prayers, concerns and questions)

SURELY, HE HAS BORNE OUR GRIEFS AND CARRIED OUR SORROWS; YET WE ESTEEMED HIM STRICKEN, SMITTEN BY GOD, AND AFFLICTED. BUT HE WAS WOUNDED FOR OUR TRANSGRESSIONS, HE WAS BRUISED FOR OUR INIQUITIES; THE CHASTISEMENT FOR OUR PEACE WAS UPON HIM, AND BY HIS STRIPES WE ARE HEALED.

ISAIAH 53:4-5

DAY 11: SURELY, HE HAS BORNE OUR GRIEFS

"Alone." That's how I often describe my feelings when going through crisis and feeling battle-weary.

"There's no one who understands." That's how I often excuse my own isolation and self-pity.

"It's not going to change anything." That's how I often brush aside my apathy.

If we refuse to be totally honest with ourselves, it does us no good to seek the Lord in the midst of crisis. And, if I'm being totally honest with myself, I'm pretty self-centered in trial, especially if I'm feeling attacked, manipulated, or unappreciated. Most parents, when feeling battle-weary in the fight to bring healing and hope to their children, feel this way. You may be feeling some of these feelings right now. It's okay. It's normal. But it's not okay to stay there.

Not only has Jesus felt these same feelings—He actually *was* rejected and *was* alone—He bore all of it so that in times like these, we would have a trusted friend to walk beside us. There was and is no one who understands more than Him. I love this quote from John Piper about Isaiah 53:4&5,

"Instead of collapsing in grief over our rejection, he bears our griefs. Instead of increasing our sorrows, he carries our sorrows. Instead of avenging our transgressions, he is pierced for them in our place. Instead of crushing us for our iniquities, he is crushed for them as our substitute. And all the chastisement and whipping that belong to us for our rebellion he takes on himself in order that we might have peace and be healed."

Wow.

He gets it. He totally does. He became all of it for you—for ME!

Today, I am so grateful for a Savior who literally carried the cross for me, for days like this one. For my sorrow, for my grief, for my loneliness, for my rejection, for my pain, and for my rebellion. I am not alone. You are not alone. Our children are not alone because God has brought them into our lives so that they will never be alone again.

Go into your child's dark place and pick up your cross for them. Remind them through your presence and love that although they may *feel* alone, they will never *be* alone again. Sometimes that means sitting quietly and doing nothing. Sometimes it means having some silly fun in a game they enjoy just to bring some laughter to their soul and respite to yours. Sometimes it means going on a walk, hand in hand, simply to communicate that you're there and that you understand. We can't walk the road of healing *for* our children, but we can clear the weeds from the path and help them to navigate.

> **"We can't walk the road of healing, for our children, but we can clear the weeds from the path and help them to navigate."**

In order to pick up our own cross for our children, we must be free to lay down our burdens before Jesus and trust that He understands. He has born your grief, He has felt your sorrow, and He has shared in your suffering on the cross. He did that so that, on days like this one, you would trust Him with your burdens. He truly understands.

Scripture Meditation: Take a few moments to read the following Scriptures. Allow the Holy Spirit to speak to your heart about each of them.

Psalms 55:22 "Give your burdens to the Lord, and he will take care of you. He will not permit the godly to slip and fall."

Psalms 145:14 "The Lord helps the fallen and lifts up those bent beneath their loads."

Galatians 6:2-5 "Share each other's troubles and problems, and in this way obey the law of Christ. If you think you are too important to help someone in need, you are only fooling yourself. You are really a nobody. Be sure to do what you should, for then you will enjoy the personal satisfaction of having done your work well, and you won't need to compare yourself to anyone else. For we are each responsible for our own conduct."

1 Timothy 5:8 "But those who won't care for their own relatives, especially those living in the same household, have denied what we believe. Such people are worse than unbelievers."

Capturing Thoughts: Throughout your adoption journey, I encourage you to capture your thoughts, fears, moments of joy, memories, and challenges. It will be a great encouragement to go back and read what you've written before. Looking back, you'll be surprised how much you and your family grow through your experiences.

Prayer Starter: Jesus, thank you for bearing my sin, sorrow, and grief. Give me the strength to carry my child's sorrow, even in the midst of their rejection and hurt. Help me to show them your love. Help me to deal with my own sorrow, hurt, and pain. Thank you for allowing me to share these burdens with this precious child you've given me stewardship over.

Discussion Questions – Day 11: Surely, He Has Born Our Griefs

1. Have you ever thought about your own sin and rebellion and reflected on Jesus' willingness to suffer on the cross so that you could be set free as a comparison to your own willingness to suffer for your child so that they can be set free? What does that perspective change for you?

2. Today's devotion says, "We can't walk the road of healing *for* our children, but we can clear the weeds from the path and help them navigate." What types of things can you do to help clear the weeds for your child?

3. Is it easy for you to lay down your worries, concerns, and burdens and trust the Lord? Why or why not?

4. Talk about a time you felt alone and someone came along and cared for you. How did that make you feel? Do you think your child feels lonely? If so, how can you come alongside them and help them feel cared for?

My Journey:

(Use this space to capture your thoughts, prayers, concerns and questions)

FOR THE WORD OF GOD IS LIVING AND POWERFUL, AND SHARPER THAN ANY
TWO-EDGED SWORD, PIERCING EVEN TO THE DIVISION OF SOUL AND SPIRIT,
AND OF JOINTS AND MARROW, AND IS A DISCERNER OF THE THOUGHTS AND
INTENTS OF THE HEART.

HEBREWS 4:12

DAY 12: THE WORD OF PROMISE

There is not a more powerful force on the face of this earth than a Christ-follower who knows how to properly weld their sword—the Word of God. I read a quote on a Facebook meme yesterday that, unfortunately, fits so many of us in times of crisis, "Complaining about a quiet God while your Bible is closed is like complaining about not getting texts while your phone is turned off." The spirit of a parent (or anyone) who's deeply invested in God's Word is hard to shake, even when they are battle-weary. We absolutely cannot win the battle for the hearts and minds of our children without a personal life in the Word of God.

It's important for you to understand that when the Bible talks about the "word" of God, it has two distinct meanings and uses, both of which are critical in crisis—and in all of life. The first word is "logos" which refers to the *complete* Word of God, the Bible in its entirety, and Jesus, its fulfillment. The second word is "rhema"—an utterance—which refers to our weapon against the enemy. A rhema word is a scripture or portion of scripture that the Holy Spirit brings to our remembrance as a weapon of faith. It's sometimes referred to as a "now" word of God, relevant and perfectly suited to the current situation in your life. We put it to use by standing on its truth, confessing it with our mouth and understanding its authority and completeness from God's word (logos).

The truth is, if your faith is weak, your word life is weak. You simply cannot have one without the other. No one else can carry our sword for us. They can lift

"Many times, my soul has been worn out and weary yet my faith in the promises of God's word remained unshaken."

us up, encourage us, and remind us of God's promises, but they cannot fight *our* battles with *their* swords. It's also important to understand that there's a big difference between a weak faith and a tired soul. Many times, my soul has been worn out and weary yet my faith in the promises of God's word remained unshaken. I've been in a position that I felt "done" with the whole situation, tired of the battle with a particular child, and desperately ready to "get past" the current behavior or season. Yet, even then, I remained steadfast in faith knowing that ultimately God's story in their lives (and mine) would prevail. But the *only* reason that I've been able to hold fast in my spirit is because I have a personal life in God's word. I would not make it otherwise.

For the battle-weary parent, there is no greater weapon than the living Word of God. The first thing that tends to go during times of trial is our personal time with God. We get busy and distracted in the battle and forget to pull away and refill our ammo. Fight hard for your time with the Lord; it's where your strategy, direction, and help come from. He has given you *the* word of promise!!!

Scripture Meditation: Take a few moments to read the following Scriptures. Allow the Holy Spirit to speak to your heart about each of them.

Psalm 119:11 "I have hidden your word in my heart, that I might not sin against you."

Joshua 1:8 "Study this Book of the Law continually. Meditate on it day and night so you may be sure to obey all that is written in it. Only then will you succeed."

Nehemiah 8:3 "He faced the square just inside the Water Gate from early morning until noon and read aloud to everyone who could understand. All the people paid close attention to the Book of the Law."

Romans 10:17 "Yet faith comes from listening to this message of good news—the Good News about Christ."

Capturing Thoughts: Throughout your adoption journey, I encourage you to capture your thoughts, fears, moments of joy, memories, and challenges. It will be a great encouragement to go back and read what you've written before. Looking back, you'll be surprised how much you and your family grow through your experiences.

Prayer Starter: God, thank you for your Word. Help me to hide it in my heart so my faith would be made strong. Thank you for the weapon of your Word in the warfare for my child at this very moment. We know that your promises are true, and we speak the life of your Word over our situation, even now. Your Word tells us that your promises are "Yes! And Amen!" to those who believe. We believe you and your promises for our family and our child.

Discussion Questions – Day 12: The Word of Promise

1. What's your biggest obstacle when it comes to carving out time to diligently read the Word? Talk about ways you can overcome that obstacle.

2. Read Joshua 1:8. What does it mean to meditate day and night on the Word?

3. Today's devotion talks about the difference between weak faith and being a tired soul. What does that distinction mean to you? Do you think you know the difference for yourself?

4. Write down two promises from God's Word for your family. Mediate on those throughout the day. Make note of how your faith increases as you put this simple practice into place.

My Journey:

(Use this space to capture your thoughts, prayers, concerns and questions)

Refrain your voice from weeping, and your eyes from tears; for your work shall be rewarded, says the Lord, and they shall come back from the land of the enemy. There is hope in your future, says the Lord, that your children shall come back to their own border.

JEREMIAH 31:16-17

DAY 13: YOUR WORK SHALL BE REWARDED

"This parenting thing isn't for the faint of heart," is something I've said over and over again at times our journey has been especially difficult. It's true. Parenting is hard work. Parenting children from hard places whose lives were greatly shaped and broken before they joined our family is especially hard work. We don't always see where the broken pieces are, and in our effort to help, sometimes get cut by a sharp edge of trauma, grief, and loss. It's comforting to know that God not only understands, but He promises that our work will be rewarded, even when it seems our children are distant and far away.

God's promises regarding our children who are distant and far away, whether physically, emotionally, or both, are comforting to me because I know that He truly does understand. He is also a Father to distant and far away children—us. All throughout scripture we witness His children coming into intimate, loving, and grateful relationship with Him only to turn away and forget all He's done for them.

> **"God's promises regarding our children who are distant and far away, whether physically, emotionally, or both, are comforting to me because I know that He truly does understand."**

He knows what it's like to reach out in love and have His efforts rejected, unappreciated, mocked, and ridiculed. Even still, He still pursues our hearts with abandon because He is our Father, and He will never give up on us.

Today's scripture gives us great hope to hold onto. It's a promise from our Father that we can set our faith on in times of difficulty with a child. At the same time, it also challenges us to limit our own self-pity. *"Refrain your voice from weeping, and your eyes from tears…"* doesn't mean that we can't grieve or feel the heartbreak of crisis with a child. It means that we can't wallow in it. We still have work to do. The rest of the verse is a complete promise from God that He's got it. We can release it to Him and trust that He will draw our children back to Himself and to us, their family. It frees us to get back to work—to our marriage, our other children, and ourselves.

With seven daughters, there have been several times in our family that we've been in crisis with multiple children at one time. Those times were exhausting and required the effort of *everyone* to get us back on track. More often than not, however, it's one child who's deeply in the muck of what I'll nicely call "stuff." Anytime we're in crisis with even one child, it's easy to stop working on our marriage, on the issues our other children might be facing, or even our own stuff because we're so focused on current battle. This is exactly what today's scripture cautions us about. We can't allow the enemy to distract us with one battle while making headway in the overall war to divide and destroy our family.

In the midst of crisis, we have to rest in God's promises to return our children from the enemy. In doing so, we put our confident trust in Him and keep our eyes focused on the ultimate battle—our entire family. This might mean that we take a weekend romantic trip with our spouse, right in the thick of it. Why? Because if our marriages aren't strong, our children aren't strong, and the enemy suddenly has a stronger foothold. It might mean that we take a day trip with the family to do something fun. Why? Because we can't allow the enemy to suck the life out of the entire household. A little laughter will do the entire family some good, especially the child in crisis.

By putting our entire life on hold in the midst of crisis, we allow the enemy to stall us. We must be sensitive to the Lord in battle-weary seasons, allowing Him to direct our steps in faith, not in fear. God's promises are given so that we can hold on in faith and trust Him to care for our children. Hold onto His Word and fight for your child and your entire family. You can have confidence that your work will be rewarded. In a spirit of trust and confidence, turn your attention to the full work of your family with contentment and joy.

Scripture Meditation: Take a few moments to read the following Scriptures. Allow the Holy Spirit to speak to your heart about each of them.

Psalm 103:17-18 "But the love of the Lord remains forever with those who fear him. His salvation extends to the children's children of those who are faithful to his covenant, of those who obey his commandments."

Psalm 127:3 "Children are a gift from the Lord; they are a reward from him."

Psalm 139:13-16 "You made all the delicate, inner parts of my body and knit me together in my mother's womb. Thank you for making me so wonderfully complex! Your workmanship is marvelous—and how well I know it. You watched me as I was being formed in utter seclusion, as I was woven together in the dark of the womb. You saw me before I was born. Every day of my life was recorded in your book. Every moment was laid out before a single day had passed."

Proverbs 22:6 "Teach your children to choose the right path, and when they are older, they will remain upon it."

Capturing Thoughts: Throughout your adoption journey, I encourage you to capture your thoughts, fears, moments of joy, memories, and challenges. It will be a great encouragement to go back and read what you've written before. Looking back, you'll be surprised how much you and your family grow through your experiences.

Prayer Starter: Father, thank you that you had a plan before my child was born, before they entered our family. You know their every hair, every thought, and every moment, and you've designed them all as a reward from you. We come into agreement with your promises that ultimately their life will glorify you, and every seed that we've sown will be watered and harvested in their life.

Discussion Questions – Day 13: Your Work Shall Be Rewarded

1. Talk about a time that you felt distant and far away from God. Even in your relational absence, do you think He gave up on you? What does this perspective mean for you as a parent in crisis?

2. Psalm 139:13-16. God knew, before your child was born, that they would become a part of your family. He also knew that this moment of difficulty would also arrive. How does this idea challenge or encourage you?

3. Do you sometimes find yourself distracted from other important relationships because you're focused on the issues with one particular child?

How can you take a step back and refocus on the bigger picture of your family?

4. What's one thing that's fallen out of focus you can immediately put back on the priority list?

My Journey:

(Use this space to capture your thoughts, prayers, concerns and questions)

WHAT THEN SHALL WE SAY TO THESE THINGS? IF GOD IS FOR US, WHO CAN BE

AGAINST US?

ROMANS 8:31

DAY 14: I AM FOR YOU

I've never had a tattoo, but if I were to ever get one it might just say, "I am FOR you!" If there's a message that I need to be reminded of on a minute-by-minute basis, it's that God is for *me*, and I am *for* my family and friends. It's so easy to get caught up in the daily grind of life and find myself defaulting to my natural desire to accuse, find fault, and cast blame—especially as a wife and mom. My husband and children have no shortage of things that need to change (as do I, by the way) and if I'm not careful, I can find myself policing their lives, constantly reminding them of their moral and behavioral shortcomings. And let's face it, no one wants to live with the warden.

There's a vast difference between a position of authority and a position of influence. This principle is as true in parenting as it is in business leadership. As the leaders of our homes, we have the privilege of setting rules, boundaries, and behavioral expectations for our families. We can choose to exercise our God-given privilege from either a position of authority or a position of influence, the difference being moral superiority and a demand to do things "my way" as opposed to relational inspiration, which paves the way for obedience through respect.

Leading by influence requires us to first look in the mirror at the reflection of our own character, humility, and teach-ability in light of the expectations we place on others around us; it means that our children choose to follow our example not because they have to but because they want to. Think about the people in life that you've chosen to follow, those to whom you've returned time and time again for advice and counsel. More than likely, the examples that come to mind are people who may or may not have ever had a position of authority over you. Rather, they are people who've had influence over you because you respect their character, success, and attitude toward life. Most likely, they are people that you've known are *for* you; they have your best interests at heart, they cheer you on, they have your back, and they comfort you when you're hurting. They love you. Unconditionally.

> **"Rather than create distance with His rebellious children, God came to them in the midst of their rebellion in the form of His only Son. He was with them and for them, just as He is for us."**

Many times, especially with a child who's difficult and in crisis, we guard our heart closely because we're afraid of getting hurt, appearing to condone whatever their behavior is, or being seen as soft. In doing so, we move out of influence in our children's lives and into authority, relying on our "position" as parent to demand change, reinforce our expectations, or simply wait it out. Creating distance in the midst of difficulty, especially when you're hurt and angry with your child, is your own natural survival response kicking in, but it's not the response of the cross. Rather than create distance with His rebellious children, God came *to* them in the midst of their rebellion in the form of His only Son. He was *with* them and *for* them, just as He is for us.

It's easier to fight the problems in our lives because we know that our Heavenly Father is *for* us. We know He wants the absolute best for us and has our best interests at heart. We know that He is fighting beside us, has patience with us, and cares deeply for us. We know this because He sacrificed His only Son on our behalf and promises us that He will love us unconditionally—for eternity. As His reflection on the earth, especially in our role as parents, we are to do the same. Our children will face no shortage of obstacles, challenges, and battles as they mature into adulthood. Their battles may seem insignificant, but we too easily forget that molehills truly did look like mountains when we were their age. They must know that we are *for* them! I tell my children regularly that I'm "on their team," "your biggest cheerleader," "your #1 fan," and other phrases that are specifically meant to help them see that I have their best interests at heart and want nothing more than to see them succeed.

People who have your best interests at heart innately have influence over you. You listen to them because you know they are listening to you. For our children to listen to us, we sometimes have to lay aside our rules, adult expectations, and boundaries so that we can connect with them at a deep, meaningful level that penetrates their heart and solidifies our influence in their lives.

Scripture Meditation: Take a few moments to read the following Scriptures. Allow the Holy Spirit to speak to your heart about each of them.

Luke 6:31 (NIV) "Do for others as you would like them to do for you."

Ephesians 4:3-6 (NIV) "Make every effort to keep the unity of the Spirit through the bond of peace. There is one body and one spirit, just as you were called to one hope when you were called; one Lord, one faith, one baptism; One God and Father of all, who is over all and through all and in all."

I Corinthians 1:10 "I appeal to you, brothers, in the name of our Lord Jesus Christ, that all of you agree with one another so that there may be no divisions among you and that you may be perfectly united in mind and thought."

Romans 15:5-7 "May the God who gives endurance and encouragement give you a spirit of unity among yourselves as you follow Christ Jesus, so that with one heart and mouth you may glorify the God and Father of our Lord Jesus Christ."

Capturing Thoughts: Throughout your adoption journey, I encourage you to capture your thoughts, fears, moments of joy, memories, and challenges. It will be a great encouragement to go back and read what you've written before. Looking back, you'll be surprised how much you and your family grow through your experiences.

Prayer Starter: Lord, thank you for being *for* us, even in our worst moments. We know you've called us to parent this child at this moment in time. Because we're answering your call, you will be faithful to give us the tools and resources we need to be successful. Help us to show our child we are always on their side. Help their heart to trust our words and learn to lean on us, even as we learn to lean on you.

Discussion Questions – Day 14: I Am For You

1. Describe a time that you truly felt like someone was *for* you? How did that make you feel? How did you feel toward that person?

2. Describe a time that you've been truly *for* your child? How can you regain that spirit with them, even in the current difficulty?

3. In today's devotion, Pam describes the difference between authority and influence. How does that resonate with you? Which type of leadership do you use most often in your family?

4. Why is it difficult to move away from authoritarian habits and into a more relational style of parenting?

My Journey:

(Use this space to capture your thoughts, prayers, concerns and questions)

I WAS WITH YOU IN WEAKNESS, IN FEAR, AND IN MUCH TREMBLING.

I CORINTHIANS 2:3

DAY 15: I AM WITH YOU

Somewhere along the way we've been lied to or have lied to ourselves. The lie is this: I have to have it all together, all the time. You may not struggle with this as much as I do, but I know this is the lie I believe on a regular basis. It causes me to keep things to myself, refuse help when offered, and generally wear a mask to hide my own insecurities and fears. That's what I love so much about this simple statement from the Apostle Paul in 1 Corinthians 2:3, "I was with you in weakness, in fear, and in much trembling." With this statement Paul acknowledges that, even in the midst of walking out his call to preach the gospel to the Gentiles, he's scared, nervous, unsure of himself, and required to rely on God because he can't do it on his own. This is freedom for me, and I hope for you. We don't *have* to have it all together. As a matter of fact, we're supposed to walk this life out with fear, weakness, and trembling. Otherwise, why would we be in need of a Savior?

Acknowledging our own insecurities and fears is simply step number one. Step number two is the bigger one—we have to tell them to others. Paul didn't just feel insecure during his time with the church of Corinth, he *told* them that he felt insecure! That's a big step and a very vulnerable one. In order to fully

> "Acknowledging our own insecurities and fears is simply step number one. Step number two is the bigger one—we have to tell them to others."

explore what holds us back from this vulnerability, we must expose a few of the other lies that partner with "I have it all together."

"We made this choice; we can't look like we don't know what we're doing."

"People will judge me if they really know what's going on."

"This is 'pure and undefiled religion,' and it's not suppose to be like *this*."

"*Their* kids are doing so well, so it must be me that's doing something wrong."

"I'm a Christian, if people see my kids doing _____, they are going to judge our family."

"I can't be weak in front of my children."

On and on, the lies stack up like a Jenga puzzle—stable until, at just the right (or wrong) moment, a crisis causes the entire thing to crumble. Forgive me, I'm from Kentucky, so I'll call this what my grandfather would—hogwash. When we examine these things, we can clearly see that it's nonsense. Yet we continually fall back on this gang of lies over and over again, all while our family is privately crumbling, and the very thing we felt God called us to feels like it's taking us out. This isn't the life that God has called us to. This lie—this pride—keeps us from real relationship with our God and our families.

We really miss out when we don't struggle *with* one another. At the end of the day, we are all fellow sojourners on this journey of life. It's healthy for our children to be with us as we grapple through hard issues. It's encouraging for them to see us search for answers, pray things through, and feel the very real emotions of the journey. Being vulnerable with them opens the door for them to be vulnerable with us. Our family should be the most solid unit of support that we each have in the world. That type of family dynamic doesn't happen by accident. It requires intentional effort on the part of the parent to cultivate an atmosphere of vulnerability and trust.

We don't have this thing figured out. We're not supposed to—and that's okay. It's actually more than okay, it's by design. The process of redemption in all of our lives takes a lifetime. In order to truly be an agent of healing in our children's lives, we must first acknowledge that we're on a healing journey of our own. Our personal healing cannot come apart from honesty and vulnerability with others, which will require us to expose the lie and choose to walk in the truth of our journey.

Here's the crux of the truth: this stuff is hard, harder than we ever imagined. We need help. This process in our own lives allows us to be *with* our children in the same way that Paul was *with* the church at Corinth—in weakness, fear, and trembling. Your children need to know that you're figuring this out *with* them. Trusted companions within your community need to understand your journey so that they can be *with* you. You need to know that He is *with* you, and, even in this, you are never alone. You don't have to do it all by yourself.

Scripture Meditation: Take a few moments to read the following Scriptures. Allow the Holy Spirit to speak to your heart about each of them.

> **Psalm 119:105 (NIV)** "Your word is a lamp for my feet and a light for my path."

> **Isaiah 41:10 (NIV)** "Don't be afraid, for I am with you. Do not be dismayed, for I am your God. I will strengthen you. I will help you. I will uphold you with my victorious right hand."

Jeremiah 29:11 "For I know the plans I have for you, says the Lord, They are plans for your good and not for disaster, to give you a future and a hope."

Zephaniah 3:17 "For the Lord your God has arrived to live among you. He is a mighty savior. He will rejoice over you with great gladness. With his love, he will calm all your fears. He will exult over you by singing a happy song."

Capturing Thoughts: Throughout your adoption journey, I encourage you to capture your thoughts, fears, moments of joy, memories, and challenges. It will be a great encouragement to go back and read what you've written before. Looking back, you'll be surprised how much you and your family grow through your experiences.

Prayer Starter: Lord, thank you for being *with* me, especially in this difficult season. Even though I'm trying to do everything the best that I can, I still sometimes feel alone and afraid. Thank you for giving me the strength I need and for upholding me in this season. I know your plans for me are good, and I thank you that you calm all my fears.

Discussion Questions – Day 15: I Am With You

1. What are some of the "I have it all together" lies you get trapped in?

2. Today's devotion says, "…we're supposed to walk this life out with fear, weakness and trembling. Otherwise, why would we be in need of a Savior?" How is the idea of admitting that you're weak challenging for you?

3. Read Zephaniah 3:17. What does it mean to you that God will calm all of your fears with His love?

4. What are some of the fears you keep hidden because you worry about what others will think? How can this group pray for you in these areas?

My Journey:

(Use this space to capture your thoughts, prayers, concerns and questions)

JESUS KNEW THEIR THOUGHTS AND SAID TO THEM, 'EVERY KINGDOM DIVIDED

AGAINST ITSELF WILL BE RUINED AND EVERY CITY OR HOUSEHOLD DIVIDED

AGAINST ITSELF WILL NOT STAND.'

MATTHEW 12:25

DAY 16: WE'RE IN THIS TOGETHER

If we aren't exceedingly careful and intentional about unity, it will be stripped away in a flurry of finger-pointing, blame-shifting, and self-serving attitudes within our homes—with us, as the parents, leading the charge. We can't just give lip service to our desire for the best interests of everyone within our family; true unity requires something much deeper and more difficult—heart-service. A heart turned toward the best interest of another is one that is soft and affectionate, without malice or resentment. This means that within the worst moments of our children's behaviors, we must keep their best interests in the forefront of our minds to guide our actions, reactions, and emotions. It's not easy, but it's essential if we're going to lead the way to unity within our homes and prevent the enemy from totally tearing our family apart.

This is extremely difficult in times of crisis, especially if the child you're at odds with is operating in defiance, disobedience, and disrespect. It's easy in those moments to stand our righteous ground until the child's behavior complies with our expectations. "You don't get this until....," "Now you've lost this......," "Until you speak to me kindly/respectfully/nicely, you're absolutely not......" You get it. We've all done it. I still default to this method of parenting by nature, if I'm not intentional about unity. The problem with this is that while it might change our children's outward behavior, it doesn't produce inward transformation. It most certainly doesn't produce unity. The child will often outwardly oblige the parent's request just to avoid or get past the consequence, but inwardly they're angry and likely to repeat the behavior.

At this point you're probably thinking that I'm advocating a consequence free atmosphere in our homes for the sake of unity. You're already conjuring up the chaos that will ensue as the troops discover that the command has gone soft. Relax. That's not what I'm saying. The issue isn't about whether different behaviors deserve consequences; every parent would agree that they do. Behavior = Consequence, good or bad. It's a fact of life, for the young and the old alike. However, more often than not we default to swift and unyielding consequence because it's quick and easy, delivering quick results. The question I'm asking is does it really deliver the *right* results, in light of a spirit of loving unity and bonding within our family?

So, let's talk about unity. What does unity look like? It starts with a heart attitude that says I'm *for* you, I'm *with* you, I have your back, and how can I help you? It's important that our children feel our hearts turned toward them at all times, especially in conflict. In conflict, it's easy for us to take a self-righteous stance that hardens our hearts and creates distance from our children. We can never forget that we're in a war. Our enemy seeks to take us completely out of the game. and if he can't succeed at turning our hearts away from Jesus, he'll settle for turning our hearts away from one another. A house divided against itself will not stand. A family caught up in conflict can easily fall prey to division through control, manipulation, backbiting, gossip, bitterness, jealousy, and selfishness. As parents we must address these issues and fight for unity in our homes, starting with our own hearts.

Guarding against the enemy's plans to divide our family starts with us, the parents. It's hard to fight when you're battle-weary, I know. But you cannot quit. Hear me. Do. Not. Quit. When you are in crisis, division is at the core. Fight with unity. Arm yourself with an ear toward the spirit, a loving heart toward your child, and all your righteous anger directed at the appropriate enemy (hint: it's not your child)—the thief who comes

"Be on your guard against your own selfish interests. Put aside your desire to get your way, be right, and be in control. Work with your children as a team and teach them to do the same."

to steal, kill and destroy. Turning a loving heart toward your child, especially in crisis, disarms the enemy's hold on their mind, will, and emotions. It doesn't feel like it, but it puts you in the driver's seat and gives you the leg-up that you need to win them in love and restore unity to your home. As a family, you are in this together. You need each other. If you think of this journey as a parents vs. kids grudge match, everyone loses and the knockout blow will destroy the entire family.

Be on your guard against your own selfish interests. Put aside your desire to get your way, be right, and be in control. Work with your children as a team and teach them to do the same. Remember that it's alright to disagree in a spirit of love. It's also alright to allow your children to experience failure, suffer natural consequences, and be imperfect. It's how they'll grow. Above all, remind your family regularly that, "We're in this together!" A house divided will not stand. So stand. Stand in unity, err on the side of love, and always—always—make sure your children know that you are their biggest fan.

◆ ◆ ◆

Scripture Meditation: Take a few moments to read the following Scriptures. Allow the Holy Spirit to speak to your heart about each of them.

Romans 2:4 "Don't you see how wonderfully kind, tolerant, and patient God is with you? Does this mean nothing to you? Can't you see that his kindness is intended to turn you from your sin?"

Luke 6:27-31 "But to you who are willing to listen, I say, love your enemies! Do good to those who hate you. Bless those who curse you. Pray for those who hurt you. If someone slaps you on one cheek, offer the other cheek also. If someone demands your coat, offer your shirt also. Give to anyone who asks; and when things are taken away from you, don't try to get them back. Do to others as you would like them to do for you. "

Leviticus 19:17-18 "Do not nurse hatred in your heart for any of your relatives. Confront people directly so you will not be held guilty for their sin. Do not seek revenge or bear a grudge against a fellow Israelite, but love your neighbor as yourself, I am the Lord."

1 Corinthians 13:4-7 "Love is patient and kind. Love is not jealous or boastful or proud or rude. It does not demand its own way. It is not irritable, and it keeps no record of being wronged. It does not rejoice about injustice but rejoices whenever the truth wins out. Love never gives up, never loses faith, is always hopeful, and endures through every circumstance."

Capturing Thoughts: Throughout your adoption journey, I encourage you to capture your thoughts, fears, moments of joy, memories, and challenges. It will be a great encouragement to go back and read what you've written before. Looking back, you'll be surprised how much you and your family grow through your experiences.

Prayer Starter: Father, you call us to unity as a family and you call us to lead our children in righteousness. Sometimes both of these are hard because they feel like they conflict. Teach us how to stand firm while remaining flexible. Give us ears to hear you and a heart that's turned toward our children in love and kindness. Thank you for having patience with us in our own sin; teach us to forgive and love like you.

Discussion Questions – Day 16: We're in This Together

1. Read Luke 6:27-31. In what ways do you struggle with turning the other cheek? In what ways does this scripture apply to your feelings and actions with your child right now or in times of conflict?

2. Today's devotion says, "Put aside your desire to get your way, be right, and in control. Work with your children as a team and teach them to do the same." Describe a conflict that you fought to get your own way only to later realize that it wasn't the best choice? How did you resolve the issue? Describe a time you worked together with someone in conflict to arrive a mutually agreeable solution? How did this type of result feel?

3. Make a list of ways that your heart is turned away from your child. Make a list of ways that your heart is *for* your child and you feel like you're in unity with them.

4. Discuss the emotions that you're struggling with that might be holding you back from unity in your family. How can this group help you to overcome those?

My Journey:

(Use this space to capture your thoughts, prayers, concerns and questions)

THEREFORE, TAKE UP THE WHOLE ARMOR OF GOD, THAT YOU MAY BE ABLE TO WITHSTAND IN THE EVIL DAY, AND HAVING DONE ALL, TO STAND.

PSALMS 40:1-3

DAY 17: YOU SHALL NOT PASS!!!

Okay, here's a little secret about me. I'm a Lord of the Rings, Star Wars and Star Trek fan. I've tried really hard not to let this nerdy part of me show up in my writings. But seriously, who can avoid a LOTR reference when talking about battling the enemy? So, here you go. If you're a Lord of the Rings fan, you undoubtedly know the scene where Gandalf the Grey faces the Balrog, a great demon of fire and flame, on the Bridge of Khazad Dum trying to escape with the fellowship of nine from the mines of Moria. As the fellowship races across the bridge to safety just on the other side, the Balrog appears behind them spreading his great wings of fire and slashing his whip-like tail of flame. Gandalf, the leader of the group, turns to face the Balrog on the narrow stone bridge. With authority he extends his arm forward, placing his staff between the Balrog on the other side of the bridge and himself. With his friends at his back running safety to the other side and his staff outstretched as he faces the enemy, he stamps his staff on the ground in front of him and declares boldly with a voice of one whose authority cannot be questioned, "You Shall Not Pass!"

As parents, on behalf of your family, your authority in the spirit cannot be questioned. You are the guardians of the gate and the buck stops with you. As the ultimate authority within the home, you absolutely must hear clearly from God when it comes to decisions about your family—especially in crisis. In the same way that Gandalf, as the leader of the group, stood with

111

authority between the Balrog and his little family of nine, you stand between your family and the enemy. We have to develop a faith-filled prayer life to guard against all of the schemes of hell directed toward our family. In a similar way that Gandalf stamped his staff on the ground we must plant our feet solidly, stomp them even, and declare boldly to the devil, "You Shall Not Pass!" Having done that, STAND!

> **"There is absolutely no question that the enemy, the thief who comes to steal, kill, and destroy has every intention of dividing our families and setting our hearts away from one another."**

I love this verse in Isaiah 59:19, "So shall they fear the name of the Lord from the west, and His glory from the rising of the sun; when the enemy comes in like a flood, the Spirit of the Lord will lift up a standard against him." There is absolutely no question that the enemy, the thief who comes to steal, kill, and destroy has every intention of dividing our families and setting our hearts away from one another. He comes into our thinking, into our actions, into our reactions, and into our emotions through bitterness, anger, resentment, and fear. The good news is this—when he attacks us, if we lean on the Lord and take our stand in His authority, we can defeat the enemy. As the scripture says, the Spirit of the Lord lifts up a standard against our enemy! A "standard" is a flag or banner that was carried ahead of the army into battle. It was used as a sign to the army where and how to fight. As long as the standard was raised, the army continued the fight and knew they were winning. So for the Spirit of the Lord to "lift up a standard" against our enemy means that we are winning, and we must continue the fight!

With the Spirit of the Lord leading, you can stand strong against the enemy, knowing you aren't fighting this battle alone. Precious moms and dads, there is no diagnosis—no RAD, no ADHD, no Bipolar, no Borderline Personality Disorder, no FAS, no ANYTHING—in which the Lord can't bring peace, understanding, and victory. There is also no crisis—no runaway, no drug addicted teen, no sexually active teen, no pregnant teen, no violent outburst, no rejection, no arrest, no ANYTHING—in which the Lord can't intervene and restore. Trust in Him for wisdom, lean on Him for understanding, allow Him to direct your steps, and rely on Him for mercy, grace, and patience in your journey. His timing is not our timing, His ways are not our ways. We must stand against the enemy and trust in the Lord, at all times. Never forget the words of Deuteronomy 31:8, "Do not be afraid or discouraged, for the Lord will personally go ahead of you. He will be with you; He will neither fail you nor abandon you." Wow. Now that's good news. Stand.

Scripture Meditation: Take a few moments to read the following Scriptures. Allow the Holy Spirit to speak to your heart about each of them.

Ephesians 6:11 "Put on all of God's armor so that you will be able to stand firm against all strategies and tricks of the devil. For we are not fighting against people made of flesh and blood, but against the evil rulers and authorities of the unseen world, against those mighty powers of darkness who rule this world, and against wicked spirits in the heavenly realms."

1 Corinthians 16:13-14 "Be on guard. Stand true to what you believe. Be courageous. Be strong. And everything you do must be done with love."

1 Peter 5:8-9 "Be careful! Watch out for attacks from the devil, your greatest enemy. He prowls around like a roaring lion, looking for some victim to devour. Take a firm stand against him, and be strong in your faith. Remember that your Christian brothers and sisters all over the world are going through the same kind of suffering you are."

John 10:10 "The thief's purpose is to steal and kill and destroy. My purpose is to give life in all its fullness."

Capturing Thoughts: Throughout your adoption journey, I encourage you to capture your thoughts, fears, moments of joy, memories, and challenges. It will be a great encouragement to go back and read what you've written before. Looking back, you'll be surprised how much you and your family grow through your experiences.

Prayer Starter: Lord, reveal to me any area the enemy is trying to gain a foothold in our family and in our child's life. I stand in agreement with your Word that no weapon formed against us will prosper. Each and every member of our family has a divine purpose in accomplishing your will upon this earth. Thank you for leading and guiding us in all wisdom that we might be aware of the enemy's tactics within our family.

Discussion Questions – Day 17: You Shall Not Pass!

1. Do you struggle with spiritual warfare? If so, discuss what holds you back from standing in the authority that is given to you in the Bible as a joint-heir with Christ.

2. In today's devotion, Pam lists many diagnosis and severe behaviors parents may struggle with. Is it hard for you to believe that God can give you strength to weather these storms and trust He will restore? Talk about what restoration looks like to you in your specific situation.

3. Can you trust God and stand firm against the enemy, even if your situation doesn't change immediately or for a very long time? Journal about your challenges with having to endure this storm for a long period of time. Use your journal entry to pray through your fears, feelings, and fatigue.

4. Choose a scripture from today's devotion to stand upon as a family. Share the scripture you chose with your group and why you chose it.

My Journey:

(Use this space to capture your thoughts, prayers, concerns and questions)

AND HE PERMITTED NO ONE TO FOLLOW HIM EXCEPT PETER, JAMES, AND JOHN, THE BROTHER OF JESUS. THEN HE CAME TO THE HOUSE OF THE RULER OF THE SYNAGOGUE, AND SAW A TUMULT AND THOSE WHO WEPT AND WAILED LOUDLY. WHEN HE CAME IN, HE SAID TO THEM, 'WHY MAKE THIS COMMOTION AND WEEP? THE CHILD IS NOT DEAD, BUT SLEEPING." AND THEY RIDICULED HIM. BUT WHEN HE HAD PUT THEM ALL OUTSIDE, HE TOOK THE FATHER AND THE MOTHER OF THE CHILD, AND THOSE WHO WERE WITH HIM, AN ENTERED WHERE THE CHILD WAS LYING.

MARK 5:37-40

DAY 18: THIS ISN'T FINAL

In our journey as parents we've had an abundance of difficult times within our family. In every instance, every single one, there have been numerous people who had opinions, ideas, and even "direction from God" on how we should deal with the situation. Sometimes their input felt right, other times it felt like the worst possible thing we could do at the moment.

Listen to me carefully. When you are in crisis with a child and you're tired, weary, and desperate for answers, it's very easy for the enemy to use even the most well-meaning person to create confusion. In crisis, we're fighting enough doubt and fear of our own, without adding outside voices to the mix. This is exactly what Jesus did in today's scripture. He only took three of His disciples, the three that He knew could stand with Him in faith and not be swayed by what they saw. When He entered the Ruler's house, the scene was filled with grieving family and friends, heartbroken because she was dead. He kicked them out. Why? Because they had already accepted her death. He kept five people with Him, the "dead" girl's mother and father and His three disciples; three who could see life with the eyes of faith and not doubt and two who refused to believe she was dead because of their great love for her.

There is a gigantic difference between those who are useful as prayer warriors in your crisis and those who are useful as walking partners and wise counsel. One will pray for you from afar, knowing only that you need prayer because your family is going through immense difficulty; the other (the few) will walk near to you as you face the fire. We need the people who walk with us to know the ins and outs of our family and give us wise counsel and support from a position of unity. Most importantly, we need people who believe it can and will work out—people of unwavering faith. You have to be careful who you let all the way in, especially when you're dealing with crisis. Remember that the issues you may be going through may be issues most people have never imagined dealing with. You cannot let someone else's uneducated and non-compassionate attitudes and opinions into your heart and mind when you're trying to walk with one of your kids through difficulty.

> **"You need to be careful who you let all the way in, especially when you're dealing with crisis. Remember that the issues you may be going through may be issues most people have never imagined dealing with."**

For example, if you're walking with your child through bouts of rage and destruction of your home, many well-meaning friends may assume that taking him out behind the woodshed and dealing with all of that disrespect is the best thing you can do. Even worse, others who don't understand why anyone would foster or adopt in the first place may counsel you to "send him back so you can rest." However those same friends may be totally ignorant of the severe abuse he suffered as a young child and the devastating effects of early childhood trauma on your precious son. If you, a son or daughter of the living God, cannot stand with him toward healing, who will?

A perfect example of someone following this principle is a dear friend of mine dealing with cancer; melanoma, one of the most deadly forms of cancer that exist. The amazing part of her story is that although she's had this diagnosis at varying degrees for more than five years, she's vibrant, happy, full of life, has a head full of gorgeous long and curly hair and is absolutely filled with faith that God's plan for her is healing. If you met her today, you wouldn't have a clue she had cancer unless she chose to tell you; she won't. I'm fully convinced she's living the abundant life she is because she follows this very principle. When she goes to the doctor, she only allows them to speak the minimal facts about her condition—no timelines, no prognoses, nothing but positivity. Her position is, "tell me what my next steps are based on the current tests and that's all." Outside of the doctor, there are only a handful of friends who know the full truth about where she is on her journey, those who are full of faith and never doubt God's healing power in her life. She surrounds herself with likeminded people; she intentionally and purposefully shuts down negative input from doctors, from people, and from the Internet. She is a shining example of the scripture from Matthew 12:30, "He who is not for me is against me, and he who does not gather with me scatters." She knows that anyone who is not totally on board with her mindset is against her mindset and will bring doubt, confusion, and sadness into her situation, emotions her mind and body have no time to entertain because all of their energies are focused on glorifying God and healing.

You are the expert. You are the gatekeeper. You are the one that God has entrusted with this precious child. Surround yourself with people of faith; don't let people who love you and mean well scatter and divide your family. Standing in faith for your family and your child means standing with the few who are willing to link arms with you, *agree* with you in prayer, and speak *life* into your situation and into your personal heart and mind.

Scripture Meditation: Take a few moments to read the following Scriptures. Allow the Holy Spirit to speak to your heart about each of them.

Proverbs 3:5-8 "Trust in the Lord with all your heart and do not depend on your own understanding. Seek his will in all you do, and he will direct your paths. Don't be impressed with your own wisdom. Instead, fear the Lord and turn your back on evil. Then you will gain renewed health and vitality."

Proverbs 12:25-26 "Worry weighs a person down; an encouraging word cheers a person up. The godly give good advice to their friends; the wicked lead them astray."

Proverbs 22:24-25 "Keep away from angry, short-tempered people, or you will learn to be like them and endanger your soul."

Proverbs 27:17 "Iron sharpens iron, a friend sharpens a friend."

Capturing Thoughts: Throughout your adoption journey, I encourage you to capture your thoughts, fears, moments of joy, memories, and challenges. It will be a great encouragement to go back and read what you've written before. Looking back, you'll be surprised how much you and your family grow through your experiences.

Prayer Starter: Jesus, help us to surround ourselves with those who are full of faith and understand our journey. Help us to discern who will lead us in your paths during this time of struggle and uncertainty. We know that our minds need to remain focused on your purposes and plans, bring friends alongside us who will stand with us in steadfast faith to see our situation through your eyes.

Discussion Questions – Day 18: This Isn't Final

1. Have you ever gotten bad advice from a friend who doesn't have any understanding of your situation? How did you discern whether to take the advice? How did you handle the situation with your friend?

2. Read the two accounts of Jesus healing in response to faith from Mark 5:21-42. How do those stories of faith encourage you in your own situation?

3. In today's devotion, it says, "Surround yourself with people of faith, don't let people who love you and mean well scatter and divide your family." Have you experienced well-meaning people's opinions and words creating division in your family? Talk about a situation in which you've been able to discern this happening, and how you dealt with it.

4. As you read the story of the dead child and her parents standing with Jesus believing she would return to life, allow it to parallel your child's situation in your mind. Can you stand with Jesus and believe that regardless of what it looks like right now, your child will return to full life and relationship with you? Find a trusted friend and share what you're believing for with them.

My Journey:

(Use this space to capture your thoughts, prayers, concerns and questions)

THEN HE TOOK THE CHILD BY THE HAND, AND SAID TO HER, 'TALITHA, CUMI,'
WHICH IS TRANSLATED, 'LITTLE GIRL, I SAY TO YOU, ARISE!' IMMEDIATELY,
THE GIRL AROSE AND WALKED, FOR SHE WAS TWELVE YEARS OF AGE.
MARK 5:41-42

DAY 19: I SAY TO YOU, ARISE!

This particular day took me several weeks to write. When I came to this portion of scripture I knew that the Lord wanted me to deal with both parts; eliminating doubt/doubters from the midst of your situation (yesterday's devotion) and speaking life (today's devotion). The second part is harder for me because it's an area that I feel like I've failed in the most as a parent. While I'm quick to tell my girls that I love them, I'm on their side, I'm praying for them, and I'm their biggest fan, I'm also quick to be critical of their decisions, use phrases like "you should have" and "why didn't you?" As they've gotten older, they've been able to articulate how those words make them feel. Reflecting back to me things like, "When you tell me I "should" do something, it makes me feel like I can't make another decision or else you won't approve and think I'm wrong." What we all must learn as parents is that understanding and wisdom from the Lord rarely come by default, they usually come through failure. The saying goes that 'hindsight is 20/20,' and in this journey, that's 100% true. In this particular attribute of the Lord, it's truly in hindsight that I have learned and am learning this lesson.

After Jesus removed all of the doubters from the room, He took the child by the hand and said to her, "Little girl, I say to you, arise!" She was 12—a preteen. Jesus didn't speak to anyone else in the room; He was speaking to the dead child. He was looking at eyes that couldn't meet his own, a heart that was non-responsive, a child who was absolutely closed off to Him—she was totally dead. Before He arrived, every single person in the room saw death. But Jesus saw something different. Even as He looked at this non-responsive child, He saw life.

How often do we feel, especially in battle-weary parenting, that we're speaking to a "dead" child? A child who's completely closed off to what we're saying, how we're trying to help, and all we're doing? It's frustrating and hurtful to reach out, to try to help, to impart wisdom, to lead the way, to parent...and be totally ignored. To look at eyes that won't connect, or worse, roll! To face a heart that's closed off to every effort being made, every word being said. Breaths that are coming in quick, sharp blows through nostrils snarled and flared. Arms crossed and body turned away. This is where we often find ourselves—staring at a child full of defiance, refusing to cooperate, full of bitterness and anger. As we square off for battle, lines get drawn, gauntlets thrown down, and arrows of strife drawn against one another.

In those moments, it's super easy to become critical, hurt, and stop engaging in life-giving conversations with/for our child. It's here that we forget that our real enemy isn't our child; it's the thief who comes to steal, kill, and destroy. We ready ourselves for battle with a defiant child and take our focus off of the battle in the Spirit that's really taking us all out. In the midst of battle, we allow the enemy to steal our joy, kill our relationship with our child, and destroy hope in our lives and the life of our child. As we square off against one another, the enemy takes a foothold and reigns in our lives in bitterness, anger, resentment, hurt, and self-righteousness. If we're not careful, we will get to the other side and realize that no one won except satan, and he's done so much damage that the repairs could take a lifetime.

We recently found ourselves right here, needing to call in biblical counsel to make sure we were making the right decisions with the right spirit, as parents. In speaking with Colleen, our Pastor who wrote the Foreword to this book, she reminded us that our daughter was designed by God to be an arrow in the hand of her Mighty King, and that, like Peter, the enemy was using this moment in her life, and in ours, to sift her like wheat. She encouraged us to help our daughter turn the arrow back in the direction that its meant to be directed, at the enemy, by speaking to the daughter that God had blessed us with and not the defiant spirit that was trying to control the situation at the moment. She was right, and this was hard. The words of wisdom that Colleen imparted to us echoed Jesus' actions in today's passage; we were to speak life into our daughter and instead of doing battle with her, we were to battle in the spirit against the vicious assignment against her and ultimately, against all of us as a family. In the natural, we were to look past our defiant daughter's rolled eyes, harsh words, and crossed arms, and speak life, even as we spoke gentle truth. To call forth the God-child within her and do battle with the real enemy controlling her.

Even as I write this day, we're still in the midst of the battle. There are actions and consequences that we've had to take as parents as a result of our daughter's choices and decisions. Yet, even in the midst of those, we're practicing love and calling out the God-child within her. "Little girl, I say to you, ARISE!" These words of our Savior, Redeemer, & King to a dead little girl ring out from deep within my Spirit as I turn my heart toward Him, focus my fight on the enemy and direct my love toward our precious daughter. His heart toward us, as His wayward children, is love. Our heart, countenance, and words toward our children should be love—even in the midst of tough parenting decisions, even in the midst of painful words and actions from our children, and especially in the midst of battle. As long as there's breath in our children's bodies, God has a plan for them! A major part of the plan for them is for us, those whom He's entrusted to steward their Spirits, to love them and lead them directly to Him. He is saying to us, as parents and authorities within the Spirit, "I say to you, ARISE!" All you may see in front of you is death, but Jesus sees life. Take up the battle with the enemy, engage in a battle to win your child's heart in love and stand strong in the knowledge

"As long as there's breath in our children's bodies, God has a plan for them! A major part of the plan for them is for us, those whom He's entrusted to steward their Spirits, to love them and lead them directly to Him."

that we war not with flesh and blood. You are not alone. You are not powerless. You can fight. You can win. Arise!

Scripture Meditation: Take a few moments to read the following Scriptures. Allow the Holy Spirit to speak to your heart about each of them.

Proverbs 15:1 "A gentle answer turns away wrath, but harsh words stir up anger."

Romans 4:17 "That is what the Scriptures mean when God told him, 'I have made you the father of many nations.' This happened because Abraham believed in the God who brings the dead back to life and who brings into existence what didn't exist before."

Ephesians 4:29 "Don't use foul or abusive language. Let everything you say be good and helpful, so that your words will be an encouragement to those who hear them."

1 Peter 3:9 "Don't repay evil for evil. Don't retaliate when people say unkind things about you. Instead, pay them back with a blessing. That is what God wants you to do, and he will bless you for it."

Capturing Thoughts: Throughout your adoption journey, I encourage you to capture your thoughts, fears, moments of joy, memories, and challenges. It will be a great encouragement to go back and read what you've written before. Looking back, you'll be surprised how much you and your family grow through your experiences.

Prayer Starter: Father, give us the words to say that would encourage our child in your ways and call forth the God-child that you've purposed. Help us to practice love and focus on fighting with the real enemy, the devil. Give us wisdom in the midst of conflict to speak to the heart of the child you've blessed us with and pray against the spirit that's trying to control the situation and divide our family.

Discussion Questions – Day 19: I Say To You, Arise!

1. In today's devotion, Pam tells a personal story about using critical words instead of encouraging words when dealing with her daughters. Do you relate to that story in parenting your own child or even with your own parents? How does Pam's story challenge or encourage you?

2. Read Ephesians 4:29. How do you define foul or abusive language? Is your definition broad enough to include critical or belittling language? In what ways have you found yourself using foul or abusive language when in conflict with your child?

3. Based on today's topic of speaking life into a child, especially in the midst

of conflict, choose a way that you can say something loving and encouraging to your child (each of your children if you have multiple). Make note in your journal about their responses to your unexpected encouragement.

4. Share your experience of speaking life into your child. How can this group pray for you in this area?

My Journey:

(Use this space to capture your thoughts, prayers, concerns and questions)

FOR I AM ABOUT TO DO SOMETHING NEW. SEE, I HAVE ALREADY BEGUN! DO
YOU NOT SEE IT? I WILL MAKE A PATHWAY THROUGH THE WILDERNESS. I WILL
CREATE RIVERS IN THE DRY WASTELAND.

ISAIAH 43:19

DAY 20: SOMETHING NEW

There are feelings of utter emptiness and total dryness in our relationship
with our child that come in the battle-weary moments. That feeling that
we've tried everything, and we're just simply tired. Done. In the midst of
the wilderness when we're lost in battle and thirsty for hope, it is sometimes
impossible to believe that change can come. But it can! The problem,
however, is that we're often looking for the wrong kind of change. If we
read today's verse carefully, we'll see that the promise isn't change as much
as it is contentment. He will make a pathway *through* the wilderness, rivers *in*
the dry wasteland. It's not a promise to take you out of your current
circumstances and plop you down in a completely new setting, poof!
Wouldn't that be nice, though? It's a promise to give you a new perspective
on your current circumstances a new way *through* the trial, a new joy *in* the
battle.

There's an old folklore tale that describes an old lady living in a vinegar
bottle who bemoans her living condition and wishes for a cottage. One day
a fairy overhears her complaining and decides to grant her wish. The
woman awakes the next day in a beautiful cottage but never thanks the fairy
and eventually bemoans the cottage and wishes for a house. The cycle
repeats over and over from house to mansion, mansion to palace, finally

resulting in the woman wishing she could rule over a kingdom. It's this final time that the fairy decides the woman is ungrateful and will never be satisfied, no matter what. So when the woman awakes the next morning, she finds herself back in her vinegar bottle. The moral of the story being that if she can't be content with her vinegar bottle, she won't be content with anything because contentment begins in the heart and isn't based on the circumstances that surround us. It's a simple child's tale that illustrates the point that Paul was making in Philippians 4:12 when he said, "I know how to live on almost nothing or with everything. I have learned the secret of living in every situation, whether it is with a full stomach or empty, with plenty or little." It's the same lesson that we, as battle-weary parents, need to learn well today—the secret of living in every situation, regardless of how things are going in our homes and with our children.

There are wastelands and wildernesses in life and certainly in parenting children through difficult circumstances, hard times, and challenging phases. I remember feeling particularly empty in a season with one of our daughters where it seemed like nothing we said or did mattered and no matter how hard we tried to show love, it wasn't received at all. She continually went to others for affection, attention, wisdom, and guidance, all the while shutting us out almost completely, and at the same time, blaming us for all of her issues. It was a hurtful and frustrating time for us and we quickly became battle-weary in trying to figure out how to deal with the issue and bring about change. One day I came across this quote in one of my favorite devotionals, Jesus Calling, "When you are

> **"There are wastelands and wildernesses in life and certainly in parenting children through difficult circumstances, hard times, and challenging phases."**

131

shaken out of your comfortable routines, grip My hand tightly and look for growth opportunities. Instead of bemoaning the loss of your comfort, accept the challenge of something new. I lead you on from glory to glory, making you fit for my kingdom. Say yes to the ways I work in your life. Trust me, and don't be afraid."

I felt as though the Lord was speaking directly to my heart about being content with the circumstance and trusting Him. Instead of returning a withholding of love to her because she was withholding love from us, I began to see the circumstance as a new challenge in my life as a parent—a challenge to love unconditionally and with mercy and grace, not expecting the slightest immediate return for my investment. As I did, the Lord began to give me joy for the relationships she was building in life, celebrating the wisdom of counsel that she had surrounding her. The truth is that I couldn't fully meet all of her needs for time, attention, and affection. We have six other daughters, jobs, and a marriage. It was unrealistic of me to expect to be the sole voice in her life. Over time we've seen major improvements in this situation, and I am so thankful; however, I know now that even if it never improved, I would still be okay.

Contentment doesn't mean you're comfortable. It doesn't mean things are "normal." It doesn't mean that you are absolutely overjoyed with your circumstances. It simply means you're at peace with allowing God to do His perfect work in your own life and in the life of your family, whatever the circumstance. Sometimes the new thing that God needs to do in our battle-weary hearts is to help us find a renewed joy and peace that passes all understanding in the midst of our trial. It's in this ever-so-beautiful way that He creates a pathway through our wilderness and a river in our wasteland. He's about to do something new! Can you see it? It's already begun.

Scripture Meditation: Take a few moments to read the following Scriptures. Allow the Holy Spirit to speak to your heart about each of them.

Psalm 62:57 "I wait quietly before God, for my hope is in him. He alone is my rock and my salvation, my fortress where I will not be shaken."

Romans 8:28 "And we know that God causes everything to work together for the good of those who love God and are called according to his purpose for them."

2 Corinthians 12:10 "Since I know it is all for Christ's good, I am quite content with my weaknesses and with insults, hardships, persecutions, and calamities. For when I am weak, then I am strong."

Philippians 4:11-13 "Not that I was ever in need, for I have learned how to get along happily whether I have much or little. I know how to live on almost nothing or with everything. I have learned the secret of living in every situation, whether it is with a full stomach or empty, with plenty or little. For I can do everything with the help of Christ who gives me the strength I need."

Capturing Thoughts: Throughout your adoption journey, I encourage you to capture your thoughts, fears, moments of joy, memories, and challenges. It will be a great encouragement to go back and read what you've written before. Looking back, you'll be surprised how much you and your family grow through your experiences.

Prayer Starter: Lord, forgive us for grumbling and complaining about our current circumstances. We know as we trust in and rely on you, our strength will not fail. Help us to be content, regardless of the storm that's swirling around us.

Discussion Questions – Day 20: Something New

1. Contentment is a struggle in every area of life, especially in today's fast-paced world. How do you struggle with contentment in your family life?

2. In what ways do you think changing your own heart-attitude and being content, even in the midst of the storm, could change your current battle-weariness?

3. Today's scripture says that God will make a pathway *through* the wilderness and create rivers *in* the dry wasteland. In what ways does the idea of staying in your struggle and finding rest bring you comfort or fear?

4. Is it a challenge for you to believe that God will do something new in your situation by simply helping to change your heart-attitude? Talk about how you feel about this within the group. How can we help you overcome your fear or encourage you?

My Journey:

(Use this space to capture your thoughts, prayers, concerns and questions)

AND I AM CERTAIN THAT GOD, WHO BEGAN THE GOOD WORK WITHIN YOU,

WILL CONTINUE HIS WORK UNTIL IT IS FINALLY FINISHED ON THE DAY WHEN

CHRIST JESUS RETURNS.

PHILIPPIANS 1:6

DAY 21: IT'S NEVER TOO LATE

Parenting is serious business. We are responsible for stewarding young lives toward mature, productive, and fulfilling adulthoods, right? It's a big deal to raise our children so that they turn out well. You know, go to college, marry the right person, stay away from drugs and alcohol, have a good relationship with us, always honor and respect authority, get a good paying job, don't steal, make good grades, save sex for marriage, never lie, keep their rooms clean, do their chores, and brush their teeth. And that's just the short list. Every parent I know has an ideal outcome in mind for their child—doctor, lawyer, athlete, family man, missionary, pastor, etc. In order for the child to accomplish that outcome, there are certain steps that need to be taken and certain behaviors that need to exist (i.e. study well, read the Bible, etc.).

Some of you may already be arguing with me, "I don't have any preconceived notions for my child's life, I simply want them to be happy." Ah, yes. Happy. And by "happy," I'm sure you mean not doing drugs, being involved in criminal

> **"Every single parent I know has an ideal outcome in mind for their child—doctor, lawyer, athlete, family man, missionary, pastor, etc."**

behavior, or hooking up with the wrong types of friends. You mean "happy" on *your* terms and by *your* standards, right? I get it. That's what I used to mean too.

Now before you slam the book closed and decide that I'm a liberal parent who lets my kids get away with anything, stop. I want my girls to be happy, too. I want them to do well, be respected, act respectful, and stay away from that list of things to avoid. I, too, want the ideal for my kids and strive to teach them the fundamentals that will help them achieve those things. On the other hand, I've simply learned (through great trial and much error) that in life there's a difference between the "ideal" and the "real deal." While we may guide our children toward the ideal in life, we absolutely must understand that the real deal is what impacts us in the day-to-day issues of parenting. The real deal is this: our children are going to mess up *real* big, and we are going to have to *deal* with it. That doesn't mean we have to co-sign on their behaviors or choices, it simply means we never give up. Ever. It's never too late.

Years ago we had a family member who was trapped in a lifestyle of alcoholism and adultery. It was heartbreaking for his wife and children and for all of the extended family, as we watched the process continue year after year without change. The situation often looked hopeless yet everyone continued to pray earnestly, especially his parents and his wife, refusing to believe anything except that God would restore him to his family and deliver him from his addictions. God did exactly that. One day while sitting on the toilet, the Holy Spirit deeply convicted his heart. He repented, and literally, was never the same again. He jokingly refers to the toilet transformation as his "on the throne" moment, the only time God could get him to be completely still and listen. Today he and his wife run a nonprofit recovery ministry for addicts and abuse victims.

To say God totally restored him and delivered him is an understatement; He performed a massive miracle. It's important to understand, though, the miracle didn't occur overnight; it took years and years of steadfast prayer and refusal to give up before his parents, his wife, or anyone in his life who was praying for him saw results. On this side of his restoration, there are now hundreds of men and women who've been healed because of his testimony and his life's work in recovery. I'm sure they are eternally grateful to those who stood in prayer along his journey.

More recently in our own journey, one of our young adult daughters was totally caught up in drugs, alcohol, sneaking out, obstinate attitudes and rebellion. After months and months of dealing with the behavior, we came to the conclusion that she could no longer live under our roof. It was one of the hardest things we've ever had to do. The situation and its accompanying worry, emotional distress, and relationship barriers were becoming too much for us to bear. Agreements had been made and broken many times; we felt like her proximity to us, our rules, our disapproval of her choices, and efforts to "help" were quite possibly making it worse. We gave her a time limit to find a place. She left that night, angry, hurt, bitter, and resentful. I barely slept, and the Holy Spirit prompted me to fast and pray. The very next day I started a water-only fast for an indefinite amount of time. On day nine of the fast, a friend called me and asked me about this particular daughter. After sharing the story, she said, "I need to call you back tomorrow." On the morning of day ten, I woke up with a release in my spirit to stop fasting. It was a little confusing because I didn't see a natural answer, however, I decided that I would fast this day and break my fast the next morning. That evening my same friend called back and told me that she felt like the Lord was prompting her to offer our daughter a job that would give her purpose and something to work for that was bigger than herself. When I called her to share the news, she broke down on the phone in tears and said, "After all I've done, I can't believe Jesus would do this for me." So much has changed since that phone call and water fast. She's found a new purpose in life and has chosen to pursue her dreams, talk about her hurt, bitterness, and resentment. She's living a healthy and fulfilling life with those around her and most of all, with Jesus at its center.

In Daniel Chapter 10, we're given the example for steadfast, persistent prayer without answer. Daniel asks the Lord for wisdom and when he doesn't receive it right away, he fasts and prays until it comes. In his example, the answer comes on the 21st day (this is where we get the idea of a 21-day fast from). After 21 days, an angel appears before him and gives him the wisdom and interpretation he's been waiting for, but before he gives him the answer, the angel shares an important message that should be just as enlightening to us today as it was to Daniel. The angel tells him that God sent him with the answer the very moment that he prayed his first prayer, but he was held up in the spirit realm by the forces of evil who didn't want Daniel to receive the interpretation. The fight was so brutal that the Archangel Michael had to come and help. It took 21 days for God's answer to Daniel's prayer to arrive, not because God was withholding it, but because the enemy was fighting against it.

Why is it that you and I think our prayers for the very lives of our children are going unheard after just a few hours or even a couple of days? Our drive-thru window, microwave culture has taken away our ability to let time pass with ease. We're impatient and disbelieving. This is where we have to change our own hearts. Let me encourage you. God *always* hears your prayers and he *always* answers them. The answer may not arrive when we like, or even *be* what we like, but there *is* an answer. God's work in your family—and mine—will be finished, the seeds He's asked you to sow will grow, and the answers you've been praying for are there. We have to stop demanding it on our own timetable and learn to trust that God has it taken care of and our job is to keep praying without ceasing because *it's never too late.*

Scripture Meditation: Take a few moments to read the following Scriptures. Allow the Holy Spirit to speak to your heart about each of them.

Isaiah 40:28-31 "Have you never heard or understood? Don't you know that the Lord is the everlasting God, the Creator of all the earth? He never grows faint or weary. No one can measure the depths of his understanding. He gives power to those who are tired and worn out; he offers strength to the weak. Even youths will become exhausted, and young men will give up. But those who wait on the Lord will find new strength. They will fly high on wings like eagles. They will run and not grow weary. They will walk and not faint."

Romans 12:12 "Be glad for all God is planning for you. Be patient in trouble, and always be prayerful."

James 1:12 "God blesses the people who patiently endure testing. Afterward they will receive the crown of life that God has promised to those who love him."

James 5:11 "We give great honor to those who endure under suffering. Job is an example of a man who endured patiently. From his experience we see how the Lord's plan finally ended in good, for he is full of tenderness and mercy."

Capturing Thoughts: Throughout your adoption journey, I encourage you

to capture your thoughts, fears, moments of joy, memories, and challenges. It will be a great encouragement to go back and read what you've written before. Looking back, you'll be surprised how much you and your family grow through your experiences.

Prayer Starter: Lord, forgive us for grumbling and complaining about our current circumstances. We know that as we trust in and rely on you, our strength will not fail. Help us to be content, regardless of the storm that's swirling around us.

Discussion Questions – Day 21: It's Never Too Late

1. Today's devotions starts with, "Parenting is serious business." Have you ever found yourself taking your role as a parent a little too seriously? How easy or difficult is it for you to let go and trust God with your children and their struggles?

2. What are some dreams that you have for your children? Are you willing to let some of them go and allow God to write their story according to His purposes, even if their story includes significant struggle?

3. Pam shares a personal story about a family member who struggled with alcoholism and adultery for years whom God restored and is now running a nonprofit recovery ministry for addicts and abuse victims. Reflect on this story and consider how his journey as an alcoholic prepared him for the purpose of God on his life. Does this idea challenge you? If so, in what ways?

4. How can you see God's redemptive plan coming to pass out of your family's current struggle? What are specific things this group can pray about for you?

My Journey:

(Use this space to capture your thoughts, prayers, concerns and questions)

THAT SAME DAY TWO OF JESUS' FOLLOWERS WERE WALKING TO THE VILLAGE OF EMMAUS, SEVEN MILES FROM JERUSALEM. AS WE WALKED ALONG, THEY WERE TALKING ABOUT EVERYTHING THAT HAD HAPPENED. AS THEY TALKED AND DISCUSSED THESE THINGS, JESUS HIMSELF SUDDENLY CAME AND BEGAN WALKING WITH THEM. BUT GOD KEPT THEM FROM RECOGNIZING HIM.

LUKE 24:13-16

DAY 22: TO BE UNSEEN

"I just wish he would understand that we're only trying to help him." "Why doesn't she recognize that we love her and just simply want the best for her?" I could write a thousand sentences just like these. Sentences full of profound disappointment and loss from parents trying with all of their might to help children who've experienced losses so unimaginable that it will take their entire lives to come to grips with it all. To be unseen, having all of your efforts discarded and ignored, is a feeling that can drive you to extreme emotions—anger, bitterness, frustration, deep hurt, resignation, and disappointment. I know, I've been there.

Here's the phrase that I've heard many times and have even repeated to other families in crisis, "You have to remember that what they're doing right now has nothing to do with you. They're reacting to a pain from someone in their life long ago. They don't even realize how much you're trying to help." Sigh. It's truth. It's also the most frustrating statement in the universe for a foster or adoptive parent because there's no answer, it just is what it is, and that's frustrating.

This is what I love about the 24th chapter of Luke. Jesus perfectly illustrates walking with someone in deep brokenness yet remaining unseen. I love the lessons in this passage so much that we're going to spend a few days immersed in it. Take a deep breath and say, "I'm walking with my child on the road to Emmaus." This seven-mile journey for Jesus and his two followers is one of brokenness, doubt, learning, and healing. As we walk alongside them on this dusty road, our feet will get dirty, dust will get kicked up and cake our skin, our mouths will taste the grittiness of the dirt and our hearts will burn with understanding. Yet we must go on.

The word Emmaus in Greek means "an earnest longing." Oh how that describes our hearts as parents. We have an earnest longing for our children to relax into our care, to accept our help, and to allow the healing work of Jesus to take place in their hearts. We have an earnest longing to be seen by them, loved by them, and accepted as their parents. To be unseen with the longing of our hearts so profound is nearly unbearable.

I was working our non-profit booth at a local church recently when a lovely, grey-haired elderly woman and her middle-aged daughter approached the booth to read our literature. As we made small talk, the elderly woman shared that our message of helping older youth who've aged out of foster care meant something to her because she was a foster child herself. She said, "They just kick them out and forget about them." Her statement, her eyes, and her demeanor all communicated to me that, even now, she walked around with deep hurt and wounds from her past. She quickly changed the topic, dismissing it as "a long time ago," but I could tell it didn't feel like long ago at all, and in that moment, it felt very real and relevant. It didn't take long for her to walk away from the table, obviously desiring to put the memories behind her and to not speak of it anymore. I wish I could sit with her over a cup of tea and hear her story. It breaks my heart to think about the deep wounds she still carries to this day. As an elderly woman, she's still walking her own broken road to Emmaus, her earnest longing for healing, trying to make sense of her story amidst doubt, confusion, and hurt. She had been unseen in her pain for so long that she has made a comfortable home there, one that she carefully guards and lets few, if any, in—to do so would be nearly unbearable.

> **"Our greatest longing is for our children to see us as their mom and dad, stepping up to the plate to care for them, protect them, love them, and enjoy life with them forever."**

To be unseen, on either side of the table, as a parent trying to help a wounded child or as a wounded child trying to navigate life amidst immeasurable grief and loss (regardless of age) is uncomfortable and nearly unbearable. Yet Jesus models this very thing for us as He walks with His followers in their grief, doubt, and confusion, allowing them to be wounded and see Him as a fellow traveler on the road to Emmaus rather than their risen Savior in whom there is healing and redemption. Our greatest longing is for our children to see us as their mom and dad, stepping up to the plate to care for them, protect them, love them, and enjoy life with them forever. Our wounded children's greatest desire is that their life had never been broken in the first place, that they could have their "real" parents be the family that you're trying to be to them. Here we are, walking together, us having the desire and ability to help them while they're totally focused on their pain and confusion, unable to see us at all. As foster and adoptive parents on our road to Emmaus, we must be like Jesus, allowing ourselves to be unseen because there's important work to be done along the way.

◆ ◆ ◆

Scripture Meditation: Take a few moments to read the following Scriptures. Allow the Holy Spirit to speak to your heart about each of them.

> **Psalm 22:24** "For he has not ignored the suffering of the needy. He has not turned and walked away. He has listened to their cries for help."

> **Psalm 23:4** "Even when I walk through the dark valley of death, I will not be afraid, for you are close beside me. Your rod and your staff protect and comfort me."

> **Romans 15:5** "May God, who gives this patience and encouragement, help you live in complete harmony with each other, each with the attitude of Christ Jesus toward the other."

> **1 Corinthians 15:58** "So, my dear brothers and sisters, be strong and steady, always enthusiastic about the Lord's work, for you know that nothing you do for the Lord is ever useless."

Capturing Thoughts: Throughout your adoption journey, I encourage you to capture your thoughts, fears, moments of joy, memories, and challenges. It will be a great encouragement to go back and read what you've written before. Looking back, you'll be surprised how much you and your family grow through your experiences.

Prayer Starter: Jesus, teach us to walk alongside our child in the way that you walked alongside your followers who did not see you. Give us the wisdom to know when to say something and when to just allow our child to grieve, hurt, doubt, and fear. Thank you that you give us patience and encouragement along the road to healing in our child's life and in the life of our family. Help us to never underestimate the power of our presence as a reflection of you.

Discussion Questions – Day 22: To Be Unseen

1. Have you ever experienced someone just being with you in a moment of deep sorrow, doubt, or fear? Talk about that experience and how it made you feel.

2. What is the number one way you feel unseen by your child? Have you forgiven them or are you holding a grudge?

3. Today's devotion says, "Our greatest longing is for our children to see us as their mom and dad, stepping up to the plate to care for them, protect them, love them and enjoy life with them. Our wounded children's greatest desire is that their life had never been broken in the first place, that they could have their "real" parents be the family that you're trying to be to them." How does that statement challenge or encourage you?

4. Are there specific ways that you can be with your child this week, in the midst of your struggle?

My Journey:

(Use this space to capture your thoughts, prayers, concerns and questions)

HE ASKED THEM, 'WHAT RE YOU DISCUSSING SO INTENTLY AS YOU WALK ALONG?' THEY STOPPED SHORT, SADNESS WRITTEN ACROSS THEIR FACES. THEN ONE OF THEM, CLEOPAS, REPLIED, 'YOU MUST BE THE ONLY PERSON IN JERUSALEM WHO HASN'T HEARD ABOUT ALL THE THINGS THAT HAVE HAPPENED THERE THE LAST FEW DAYS.' 'WHAT THINGS?' JESUS ASKED.

LUKE 24:17-19

DAY 23: BROKEN PLACE TO BROKEN PLACE

There is absolutely nothing in this life that has brought out my own deep brokenness more than my journey as a foster and adoptive mom. Alcoholism, violence, emotional trauma, mental illness, unknown biological father, parental promises made and broken, death of a sibling—these things touched my life, hurt me, and shaped me into the person that I am today. As I walk beside my children, immersed in their stories, my own story is poked and prodded, not always in pleasant ways. As I sit quietly in the passage of scripture from Luke 24 where Jesus walks with His followers on the road to Emmaus, I'm reminded of my own journey. I'm also reminded that my own personal healing came (and is continuing) over the course of my life. The people who've made the biggest difference for me really haven't "done" anything, they have simply been there with me on the long road of life—loving me, listening to me, and letting me walk it out. Along my path of personal emotional healing and my journey as a mom to seven beautiful daughters who live life with the scars of loss hidden just beneath the surface, I've learned that these broken places are the most difficult to endure. To walk silently with someone (or be the someone) in grief, in emptiness, in questioning, in fighting, and in fear is the hardest road any of us ever walk in life. We are fixers. We are parents, teachers, practitioners, and friends who define our role as helpers, and helping means fixing. It means having the answers, solving the pain, and healing the wound. However, we are also the wounded. We think our helplessness is weakness, our questioning is faithlessness, our emptiness is shameful, and our fear is cowardly. We are both the fixers and those in need of fixing, and we are both wrong. The truth is simply that we are all fellow journeymen walking alongside one another from broken place to broken place. We are broken people leading broken people. We are all on the long road home.

> **"To walk silently with someone (or be the someone) in grief, in emptiness, in questioning, in fighting, and in fear is the hardest road any of ever walk in life."**

Here, in this passage of scripture, Jesus models this journey with one another through brokenness in one of the most beautiful passages that I can find in scripture. He joins two of His followers on the road to Emmaus on the day of His resurrection. For the followers, Cleopas and His friend, the long road home was a seven-mile journey between Jerusalem and a village called Emmaus. It was a walk filled with questioning, grief, emptiness, and fear. As they walked along, a "stranger" joined them and asked about their sadness. I absolutely love the way Jesus approaches this! He doesn't say, "You're wrong for being so sad." He doesn't get frustrated and hurt because they're basically thinking that He lied to them all along. He doesn't say, "After all of the time I spent pouring into you, *this* is what I get?" No, He doesn't do any of that. He simply notices their sadness and makes room for their story.

They began to share with Him the events that had unfolded over the past few days. Can you imagine their disbelief? Their wonder at whether they had been lied to all along? Their disappointment that their "family" members, a once close-knit band of brothers, were now scattered throughout Jerusalem by the death of their leader, all of them struggling to come to grips with their abandonment, rejection, grief, and loss? As they shared these things, Jesus listened. He made space for them to openly discuss their sadness. He didn't try to fix it or challenge their feelings. He simply listened, invited them to share, and provided an open forum for them to talk out the despair that was deep within their hearts. The way Jesus walked with these two broken followers is a key for all of us as parents walking the road of healing with our children. He could have come right out and told them who He was and how wrong they were in their assessment of their situation. He didn't. He listened because their feelings were real, even if they weren't necessary in light of the truth that was walking alongside them.

Too many times in my journey as a mom I've tried to "fix" my girls' feelings. To try and "fix" it totally invalidates their feelings and often communicates a "you're wrong and stupid for feeling this way" message. Jesus didn't model this as He walked with His followers in their questioning and grief for very good reason. He didn't want to teach them that they needed others to "fix" them; instead, He modeled for them the beauty of brokenness that's found in the struggle. Jesus allowed them to struggle through feelings of despair and in doing so, He gave them room to discover healing for themselves and come to terms with their own inner battles, doubts, and fears. He did it without guilt and shame and without just outright giving the answer. C'mon, think about that for a second. He *was* the answer!

There are things in all of our lives that no one can fix; they can only walk along side us as we process, grow, grieve, and learn. As we walk with our children from broken place to broken place, we must remember that we, too, are on the long road home toward healing. The same grace, time, and care that we've needed in our own journey, they need too. Let our highest goal not be to be "good, responsible parents" but to be much higher—to be good walking partners on the long road home.

Scripture Meditation: Take a few moments to read the following Scriptures. Allow the Holy Spirit to speak to your heart about each of them.

Exodus 3:7 "Then the Lord told him, 'You can be sure I have seen the misery of my people in Egypt. I have heard their cries for deliverance from their harsh slave drivers. Yes, I am aware of their suffering."

1 Samuel 1:10 "Hanna was in deep anguish, crying bitterly as she prayed to the Lord."

Psalm 25:16-18 "Turn to me and have mercy on me, for I am alone and in deep distress. My problems go from bad to worse. Oh, save me from them all! Feel my pain and see my trouble. Forgive all my sins."

Ecclesiastes 3:1-4 "There is a time for everything, a season for every activity under heaven. A time to be born and a time to die. A time to plant and a time to harvest. A time to kill and a time to heal. A time to tear down and a time to rebuild. A time to cry and a time to laugh. A time to grieve and a time to dance."

Capturing Thoughts: Throughout your adoption journey, I encourage you

to capture your thoughts, fears, moments of joy, memories, and challenges. It will be a great encouragement to go back and read what you've written before. Looking back, you'll be surprised how much you and your family grow through your experiences.

Prayer Starter: Father, give us the ability to allow our child to experience the fullness of their sorrow so that their hearts can turn to you for healing. Forgive us for times we've tried to stand in your place and heal their pain. Draw our child's heart toward you in times of deep distress, and in their struggle, show them your peace. Give us eyes to discern the seasons in our child's life and ears to hear your instruction on how we are to be with them in their journey toward you.

Discussion Questions – Day 23: Broken Place to Broken Place

1. Has a conflict with your child ever triggered your own emotions around a personal wound? How did you overcome it? What did you learn about yourself that you can share with this group?

2. What's the hardest thing for you about the idea of allowing your child to endure their suffering without "fixing" it?

3. Read Ecclesiastes 4:1-4. What times and seasons do you see in your current struggle with your child? What times and seasons do you see in your own battle-weariness?

4. In today's scripture, Jesus models noticing the sadness of His followers and making room for their story. In what way can you notice your child's sadness this week and make room for their story?

My Journey:

(Use this space to capture your thoughts, prayers, concerns and questions)

'WHAT THINGS?' JESUS ASKED. 'THE THINGS THAT HAPPENED TO JESUS, THE MAN FROM NAZARETH,' THEY SAID, 'HE WAS A PROPHET WHO DID POWERFUL MIRACLES, AND HE WAS A MIGHTY TEACHER IN THE EYES OF GOD AND THE PEOPLE. BUT OUR LEADING PRIESTS OTHER RELIGIOUS LEADERS HANDED HIM OVER TO BE CONDEMNED TO DEATH, AND THEY CRUCIFIED HIM. WE HAD HOPED HE WAS THE MESSIAH WHO HAD COME TO RESCUE ISRAEL. THIS ALL HAPPENED THREE DAYS AGO. THEN SOME WOMEN FROM OUR GROUP OF HIS FOLLOWERS WERE AT HIS TOMB EARLY THIS MORNING, AND THEY CAME BACK WITH AN AMAZING REPORT. THEY SAID THAT HIS BODY WAS MISSING, AND THEY HAD SEEN ANGELS WHO TOLD THEM JESUS WAS ALIVE! SOME OF OUR MEN RAN OUT TO SEE, AND SURE ENOUGH, HIS BODY WAS GONE, JUST AS THE WOMEN HAD SAID.' THEN JESUS SAID TO THEM, 'YOU FOOLISH PEOPLE! YOU FIND IT SO HARD TO BELIEVE ALL THAT THE PROPHETS WROTE IN THE SCRIPTURES. WASN'T IT CLEARLY PREDICTED THAT THE MESSIAH WOULD HAVE TO SUFFER ALL THESE THINGS BEFORE ENTERING HIS GLORY?" THEN JESUS TOOK THEM THROUGH THE WRITINGS OF MOSES AND ALL THE PROPHETS, EXPLAINING FROM ALL THE SCRIPTURES THE THINGS CONCERNING HIMSELF.'

LUKE 24:19-27

DAY 24: DISCOVERING TRUTH

"You're going to be adopted!" "You're going to a new home with an amazing family who will love you and take care of you." "You're finally going to have a mom and dad." These are all statements that, at one time or another, all of our children have heard. In our minds this is all good news. I mean, *we* are a good family, right? We *are* going to love them and take care of them, right? We *are* the caring, loving, responsible, safe, *chosen* mom and dad that they didn't have before us, right? So how, after all they've been through, all they've seen, and all they know about us, could they possibly doubt our role in their life and be so bitter, resentful, and rebellious? How could they possibly question everything after all we've done? So often we find ourselves in a situation similar to Jesus in this scripture, except we don't have the right to consider ourselves Saviors because He is the only Savior who has ever existed or ever will exist.

> **"We are not our children's saviors and we haven't rescued them—Jesus is and has. Just like He rescued us."**

I'll go off-script here briefly and challenge you to evaluate your motives for entering the foster and adoption process, especially if you feel like a "savior" to your children, like you've "rescued" them from a horrible situation and deserve their gratitude in return. I address motives in foster care and adoption more fully in my first book, *Ready or Not for Families Growing Through Foster Care and Adoption*. If you struggle with this idea of rescue, this savior-mentality, I encourage you to read it. God has a different journey for us, a totally different set of motivations and expectations that we should explore. We are not our children's saviors and we haven't rescued them—Jesus is and He has. Just like He rescued us. God's design for us is exactly what we see Jesus modeling here; we are to join our children as strangers along their road toward healing and walk with them as they discover the truth along the way.

Now, back to our journey with Jesus on the road to Emmaus. Here He is, the risen Savior, listening to these two followers as they recount their hopes for Jesus, their viewpoint of Him, their disappointment in His crucifixion and even the current idea that He has risen that (obviously) they're doubtful about. As they share their story, He allows them to pour it all out—their doubt, fear, questions, disappointment, and hurt—all without revealing Himself to them and letting them know that they were concerned about nothing. Why? Because our human emotions are big and they need space to air out. Sometimes we just need the room to speak the things that are in our heart without answer, without challenge, and without judgment so we can hear ourselves and begin to discover the truth on our own. We are not built to hide our emotions. We are built to work them out, to make sense of them, and to acknowledge them, even when they are wrong. Jesus gave His followers the space to share their story so they could come to grips with the ability of their own hearts to doubt, question, and fear. This is a key part of the journey of brokenness. To understand the brokenness of others, we must first discover it within ourselves. This is true empathy, feeling the pain of someone else with deep understanding. Each of us must face the depth of our own bitterness, the chasm of our own grief, and the darkness of our own doubt. If we never face it, if we never give it voice, we will never make sense of it and heal.

In our journey as parents, we've walked this process out many times. Not always successfully. Giving our daughters space to voice the emotions rattling around in their hearts often results in a vomiting of hurtful words toward us. It isn't always comfortable, and in many cases, their assessment of us as parents is simply wrong. They don't have the perspective and wisdom of a parent or the understanding of what it takes to make a family work; so, of course they're going to be off in their judgments. However, this doesn't make their feelings any less real to them, they just lack the proper understanding of the big picture. It's in these times that we have an opportunity to both give space to their story and bring understanding of the bigger picture. Jesus shows us how to make that transition as He begins to connect the dots in His followers' stories and the bigger picture of the gospel.

As Jesus began to unveil Scripture to His followers, He did so slowly and He started from the beginning. If He had began with, "I AM," He would have totally taken away their opportunity to learn. If He had started with, "Guys, seriously, can't you see that it's me? There's no need for all of this sadness and doubt. Stop worrying. Be happy. I'm here now...let's just get over the past and move forward..." they wouldn't have known the depth of their own emotions nor the depth of scripture and its eternal truth of who He is as our Lord and Savior. Their need to understand brokenness and learn the fullness of the gospel was critical to the growth of the Church for future generations. This walk to Emmaus was critical to you and I becoming adopted sons and daughters of Christ and understanding the depth of His love for us. Their brokenness was necessary so that our brokenness could be healed. The reason the gospels are timeless today is because He allowed His disciples to walk it out yesterday.

For our own comfort, we want to move our children quickly toward healing because "we're here now" so they should "stop worrying" and "get over the past." It's hard to have the answer or see a way past the current situation and not scream it at the top of our lungs so that we can all just move on and get back to our comfortable lives and routines. We must be careful, however, not to shortcut the lessons that desperately need to be learned because later in our children's journey, or maybe even our own, someone will come along who simply needs another person who truly understands. Instead of starting with "get over it, we're here now" let's start where Jesus did, "Explain what you're talking about to me so that I can understand" (Pam paraphrase). Let's move to the place where we're comfortable walking with our children *to* the answer rather than feeling like we have to *have* the answer. You never know, we may learn a few things along the path of discovering truth.

Scripture Meditation: Take a few moments to read the following Scriptures. Allow the Holy Spirit to speak to your heart about each of them.

Colossians 3:12-15 "Since God chose you to be the holy people he loves, you must clothe yourselves with tenderhearted mercy, kindness, humility, gentleness, and patience. Make allowance for each other's faults, and forgive anyone who offends you. Remember, the Lord forgave you, so you must forgive others. Above all, clothe yourselves with love, which binds us all together in perfect harmony. And let the peace that comes from Christ rule in your hearts. For as members of one body you are called to live in peace. And always be thankful."

James 1:19-20 "Understand this, my dear brothers and sisters: You must all be quick to listen, slow to speak, and slow to get angry. Human anger does not produce the righteousness God desires."

2 Timothy 2:24-26 "A servant of the Lord must not quarrel but must be kind to everyone, be able to teach, and be patient with difficult people. Gently instruct those who oppose the truth. Perhaps God will change those people's hearts, and they will learn the truth. Then they will come to their senses and escape front he devil's trap. For they have been held captive by him to do whatever he wants."

Proverbs 16:32 "Better to be patient than powerful; better to have self-control than to conquer a city."

Capturing Thoughts: Throughout your adoption journey, I encourage you to capture your thoughts, fears, moments of joy, memories, and challenges. It will be a great encouragement to go back and read what you've written before. Looking back, you'll be surprised how much you and your family grow through your experiences.

Prayer Starter: Lord, give us the wisdom and patience to give space to our child's story and their intense emotions. Forgive us for where we've moved to quickly to solve an issue or correct a problem rather than allowing you to work it out within our child. Grant us a Spirit of Empathy so that we can walk alongside our children toward healing, regardless of where the road is leading.

Discussion Questions – Day 24: Discovering Truth

1. Do you allow your child the space to share their story, even the parts of it in which they feel you contributed hurtfully?

2. What is your biggest takeaway from this walk toward Emmaus story? How do you feel about how Jesus handled his follower's doubt, disappointment, and fears?

3. 2 Timothy 2:24-26. How does this passage of scripture minister to you in this season of difficulty with your child?

4. In today's scripture, Jesus models patiently teaching his followers in the midst of their doubt, fear, and hurt, even though they were wrong in their perception of the events. Talk about ways you have or can model this with your child.

My Journey:

(Use this space to capture your thoughts, prayers, concerns and questions)

BY THIS TIME THEY WERE NEARING EMMAUS AND THE END OF THEIR JOURNEY.
JESUS ACTED AS IF HE WERE GOING TO GO ON, BUT THEY BEGGED HIM, 'STAY
THE NIGHT WITH US, SINCE IT IS GETTING LATE.' SO HE WENT HOME WITH
THEM.

LUKE 24:28-29

DAY 25: INVITING US TO STAY

The longest and most uncertain part of our journey as foster and adoptive parents is this: allowing our children the space to arrive at the conclusion that they not only need us in their life (provision) but they want us in their life (relationship). There isn't a written guarantee that our children, even biological ones, are going to grow up and value their relationship with us as their parents. For that desired outcome, there is only one path that has more certainty than all others—the path of empathy. Empathy, real empathy, gives space to the story of our children, and it doesn't try to take away their ability to feel hurt, their need to be angry, their capacity to doubt, their desire to lash out, and their instinct to push us away. The path of empathy is long, messy, and hard. Empathy in relationship, any relationship, does more than correction or control ever will. Empathy listens well, it understands readily, and it instructs compassionately.

Many times in my own journey I've bemoaned the fact that my children will go to others with their problems, and I often hear other parents do the same. We're the ones providing the roofs over their heads, clothes on their backs, and food in their bellies. Even so, they run off to Sally Sunshine down the street and tell her everything about their life and take every word she says as the gospel truth, even if she says the same thing we've said a million times. Honestly, it's more than a little frustrating at times. Why do they do it? It's simple. We can be terrible listeners, weary if they're rehearsing their past again for the millionth time, quick to judge their emotions rather than allow them to just be, offended at their unresolved anger that's directed at us, and determined to help them snap out of it so that we can move on with a normal life. This can be especially hard when we're parenting in crisis, and the child we love so dearly and tried so hard to help has opted out of relationship with us totally but talks freely with other people who have absolutely no clue how much has gone on in their life, or ours, along the way.

This is where we have to allow ourselves to correct our own behaviors and ask ourselves how well we've really walked alongside our children on their road to healing. If you're anything like me, and I hope not, you're probably not going to like much of what you discover. To walk the path of empathy, we are forced to ask ourselves, "If I were [insert child's name], would I *want* to be in relationship with me?" This is a question that requires deep understanding of relationship. The relationships we *choose* to be in are those that we enjoy, those where we feel heard, where we have fun, and with whom we are comfortable. Are we really those kind of relationships for and with our children? In truth, maybe not. And that might be okay for the moment, or it might not. Honestly, children aren't always supposed to like their parents, and we aren't suppose to be their best friends until later in life. However, there's a big difference in the normal parent/child relationship barriers and the big ones that cause our children to walk away completely and us to give up totally. Only you can decide where you fall in your relationship.

As Jesus walked along the road to Emmaus with His two followers, He did several things: He inquired about their sadness, He listened well, He didn't try to fix the issue, He didn't give them the answer, He allowed them to work out their own story, and He gently led them to truth, slowly and over time. In other words, they felt heard, understood, and enlightened with Him. He walked the path of empathy with them. As a result, when it came time that their paths could part, they invited him to stay. As a matter of fact, they begged Him to stay. Why? Because they couldn't imagine being out of relationship with Him, never seeing Him again, never getting to hear His wisdom, benefit from His counsel, or enjoy His company. They felt this way because He created an environment in which they felt valued and free to be themselves, even the darkest parts of themselves.

As the mom of seven young adult daughters, trust me when I say there will come a day when your children will have a choice in their relationship with you. As adults, they will have the power to move on and opt out of your family, to build their own life, wrestle with their own stuff, and move on. I can't imagine that you dream of a day when your Thanksgiving table has empty chairs silently reminding you of a broken relationship with your beloved child. This journey isn't easy for any of us. There will come a time, sooner than you imagine, when our children's need for us (provision) is no longer necessary in their lives, and the only thing we can hope is their want of us (relationship) is strong. As parents, walking partners in life alongside children, we must walk the path of empathy and understanding so when the natural time comes for our relational paths to go separate ways, they will happily invite us to stay.

> **"There will come a time, sooner than you can imagine, when our children's need for us (provision) is no longer necessary in their lives, and the only thing we can hope is their want of us (relationship) is strong."**

Scripture Meditation: Take a few moments to read the following Scriptures. Allow the Holy Spirit to speak to your heart about each of them.

Romans 12:14-18 "Bless those who persecute you. Don't curse them; pray that God will bless them. Be happy with those who are happy, and weep with those who weep. Live in harmony with each other. Don't be too proud to enjoy the company of ordinary people. And don't think you know it all! Never pay back evil with more evil. Do things in such a way that everyone can see you are honorable. Do all that you can to live at peace with everyone."

1 Peter 3:8-9 "Finally, all of you should be of one mind. Sympathize with each other. Love each other as brothers and sisters. Be tenderhearted, and keep a humble attitude. Don't repay evil for evil. Don't retaliate with insults when people inset you. Instead, pay them back with a blessing. That is what God has called you to do, and he will grant you his blessing."

Micah 6:8 "No, o people, the Lord has told you what is good, and this is what he requires of you: to do what is right, to love mercy, and to walk humbly with your God."

Galatians 6:1-3 "Dear brothers and sisters, if another believer is overcome by some sin, you who are godly should gently and humbly help that person back onto the right path. And be careful not to fall into the same temptation yourself. Share each other's burdens, and in this way obey the law of Christ. If you think you are too important to help someone, you are only fooling yourself. You are not that important."

Capturing Thoughts: Throughout your adoption journey, I encourage you to capture your thoughts, fears, moments of joy, memories, and challenges. It will be a great encouragement to go back and read what you've written before. Looking back, you'll be surprised how much you and your family grow through your experiences.

Prayer Starter: Father, examine our hearts for any mindset, behavior, or sin that's keeping us from walking alongside our children on their road to healing. Give us the understanding of how to have solid Christ-centered relationship with our children, regardless of their current behaviors or circumstances. Bring healing to the broken places in our relationship with our children so that we can enjoy a long life of connected relationship.

Discussion Questions – Day 25: Inviting Us Stay

1. In today's devotion, Pam says, "There will come a time, sooner than you imagine, when our children's need for us (provision) is no longer necessary in their lives and the only thing we can hope is that their want of us (relationship) is strong. What emotions, fears and challenges does this statement create for you?

2. Think about the current difficulty you have with your child. How can you better empathize with what they're feeling and experiencing?

3. Romans 12:14-18. What does it mean for you to live out this scripture within your current situation?

4. Talk about what empathy and understanding mean to you. Share a personal story with the group of a time you've experienced empathy or understanding shown to you.

My Journey:

(Use this space to capture your thoughts, prayers, concerns and questions)

AS THEY SAT DOWN TO EAT, HE TOOK THE BREAD AND BLESSED IT. THEN HE BROKE IT AND GAVE IT TO THEM. SUDDENLY, THEIR EYES WERE OPENED, AND THEY RECOGNIZED HIM. AND AT THAT MOMENT HE DISAPPEARED! THEY SAID TO EACH OTHER, 'DIDN'T OUR HEARTS BURN WITHIN US AS HE TALKED WITH US ON THE ROAD AND EXPLAINED THE SCRIPTURES TO US?' AND WITHIN THE HOUR THEY WERE ON THEIR WAY BACK TO JERUSALEM. THERE THEY FOUND THE ELEVEN DISCIPLES AND THE OTHERS WHO HAD GATHERED WITH THEM WHO SAID, 'THE LORD HAS REALLY RISEN! HE APPEARED TO PETER!'

LUKE 24:30-34

DAY 26: IN THE RIGHT TIME

Listen carefully. You have done a good job, even if you've messed up along the way. You've planted seeds, sown love, modeled family, and given beyond yourself, day in and day out. At this moment in this crisis, you may not see the answers, but the answers *will* come. Maybe not today, maybe not tomorrow, but they will come. Modeling unconditional love may take a lifetime, but you know what? That's why God's given us a lifetime to live. There are going to be seasons of difficulty in our relationships with our children, maybe even long seasons of separation. Our heart-attitude in the midst of a season of crisis, even separation, must remain fixed on hope and rest in the knowledge that, in the right time, God will restore our family.

I love the ending to the story of Jesus' walk to Emmaus with His two followers. By the time they realized who He was, He was gone. This is a big deal so listen closely. He didn't stick around to watch them celebrate who

He had been in their lives, and who He continued to be. He didn't hang around to watch them come to grips with their own healing; He was comfortable knowing that they would arrive at healing with His presence. He had sown seeds of truth into their hearts as they journeyed together, and He was okay with them blossoming after He was gone. He didn't look at them knowingly and demand an apology for all of their doubt, questioning, and unbelief. He was simply gone, comfortable knowing that everything He had done in their life would come to fullness, in the right time.

One of our daughters with whom we've had long periods of separation from time to time (residential treatment, moving away to live with birth family, etc.) recently posted a status that talked about how much she appreciated our role in her life. She articulated, for the first time ever, that we have modeled unconditional love for her no matter what she's "put us through." These were the words she chose to use out of the blue and on her own, and they greatly touched my heart. We went "through" many crises in our journey as her parents, praying for her, crying for her and with her, and loving her near and from afar as long as it took for God's story in her life to take root. Some time ago in her journey the Lord had revealed to me that He was writing the story of her life, and although I play an important role, I am not the author and therefore, can't control the script. I have no idea what His plans are for her life, nor do I know the journey she has to walk to get there. Thankfully, neither are my jobs. My responsibility is to be a good walking partner for her, to love her unconditionally, and to stay humble and steadfast before the Lord on her behalf. Honestly, that alone is a big enough job.

Another of our daughters recently married a wonderful young man. He has been her best friend for a long time and has walked with her through many struggles. She and I were talking one day and she said, "He has really helped me to process a lot of what's happened in my life. I've experienced a lot of healing through our relationship." For a brief moment, I became offended she wasn't saying that about my role in her life and by giving him that credit, she was implying that I didn't help her in that way. When the thought entered my head, I instantly knew it was a lie because in truth, I had helped her. What happened to me in that moment was that the classic enemy of foster and adoptive parents, the need to rescue, was challenged because someone else was getting hero status in her story. However, in my own story I know there have been many heroes, people who've walked with me for a season, and those who've walked with me for most of my life. None are more or less valuable than others, each having a specific role to plant a specific seed at a specific time. For all of my own heroes, I'm eternally grateful. As parents, we must, give our children room to develop those same relationships with others, whether they be future husbands/wives, therapists, teachers, or friends. It takes a village to raise all of us.

We can too easily get frustrated in our journey with others, especially our wounded children, when we don't see answers or change. It often feels like healing is taking too long or that they're refusing to accept the truth that we're trying to sow (or shove) into their lives. Like Jesus, we must become comfortable with the seeds we sow and trust that God will reveal the truth to them and allow them to see its fullness in the right time. The hard truth is we might not even be around when it happens. We are *all* on a path to healing, to restoration, and to the fullness of the knowledge of

> **"It often feels like healing is taking too long or that they're refusing to accept the truth that we're trying to sow (or shove) into their lives."**

Christ in our lives. Let's give ourselves, our kids, and others a break on the journey of brokenness. For all of us, it's a long road home.

Scripture Meditation: Take a few moments to read the following Scriptures. Allow the Holy Spirit to speak to your heart about each of them.

Psalm 37:23-25 "The Lord directs the steps of the godly. He delights in every detail of their lives. Though they stumble, they will never fall, for the Lord holds them by the hand. Once I was young, and now I am old. Yet I have never seen the godly abandoned or their children begging for bread."

Proverbs 16:9 "We can make our plans, but the Lord determines our steps."

Jeremiah 29:11-14 "'For I know the plans I have for you,' says the Lord. 'They are plans for good and not for disaster, to give you a future and a hope. In those days when you pray, I will listen. If you look for me wholeheartedly, you will find me. I will be found by you,' says the Lord. 'I will end your captivity and restore your fortunes. I will gather you out of the nations where I sent you and bring you home again to your own land.'"

1 Corinthians 3:7-9 "It's not important who does the planting, or who does the watering. What's important is that God makes the seed grow. The one who plants and the one who waters work together with the same purpose. And both will be rewarded for their own hard work. For we are both God's workers. And you are God's field. You are God's building."

Capturing Thoughts: Throughout your adoption journey, I encourage you to capture your thoughts, fears, moments of joy, memories, and challenges. It will be a great encouragement to go back and read what you've written before. Looking back, you'll be surprised how much you and your family grow through your experiences.

Prayer Starter: Jesus, thank you for making a way to bring us into relationship with our Father. Give us the wisdom to make a way for our children to come into relationship with others who will shape and guide them in Your ways. Strengthen us to allow the seeds that we've sown time to grow, be watered and come to harvest. Correct and guide us when we're trying to speed up your work in our own lives and in the lives of our children.

Discussion Questions – Day 26: In the Right Time

1. Talk about different seasons and people who made an eternal difference in your life. Did those individuals or experiences take away from or add to the influence your parents have had on you?

2. Read Jeremiah 29:11-14. The passage is talking about restoring the nation of Israel. Apply this to the restoration of your family. How does this encourage you?

3. Make a list of positive relationships in your child's life. How can you make room to allow those relationships to strengthen?

4. Talk about your own road toward healing. Take time to share with the group how God has restored and redeemed you. How does your own story give you hope for your child? Have you shared it with your child? Why or why not?

My Journey:

(Use this space to capture your thoughts, prayers, concerns and questions)

AND LET US NOT GROW WEARY WHILE DOING GOOD, FOR IN DUE SEASON WE SHALL REAP IF WE DO NOT LOSE HEART.

GALATIANS 6:9

DAY 27: DON'T GROW WEARY

I'm tired. Even as I write this, I feel weary, worn out, and just tired. Our last child graduated high school a few days ago and all of our girls are fighting through rough seasons in their lives. Adulting is hard work! Getting to this place of "freedom" hasn't been as easy as we thought, and honestly, the "freedom" hasn't actually been near as freeing as they always said it would be. I'm not sure who "they" are but when I find them, I'll sternly inform them that they've been wrong on so many things, including but not limited to "just wait until they're 18, it'll be so much easier then." Yeah…right.

As I reflect on what it means to "not grow weary while doing good," I'm reminded that as with anything, we have a tendency to skip to the end. "Just keep going until they're 18." "They'll sleep through the night by 8 weeks." "After they graduate kindergarten/jr. high/high school/college, it'll change." The list goes on and on. There's always something better out there, just over the horizon—if we can just make it through this season. In many ways, I've often read this particular scripture in the same mindset, skipping to the end, "in due season we shall reap if we faint not." So, I put the imaginary paper bag to my mouth, breathe deeply, and say over and over, "don't faint, don't grow weary…don't faint, don't grow weary." However, I don't think "keep going and push through" is really what Paul was trying to communicate here. So, for the moment, I'll put aside my paper bag and look at my own weariness in a new light. To do so, we need to back up a couple of verses.

"Don't be misled—you cannot mock the justice of God. You will always harvest what you plant. Those who live only to satisfy their sinful nature will harvest decay and death from that sinful nature. But those who live to please the Spirit will harvest everlasting life from the Spirit. So let's not get tired of doing what is good. At just the right time we will reap a harvest of blessing if we don't give up." **Galatians 6:7-9**

Wait a second! Paul is really talking about walking in our own strength here. This isn't a "push through it" verse at all, it's a STOP IT verse. Stop trying to do it all and make it all work out according to your plan. Just stop it. I don't know about you, but I spend a lot of time focusing on how I want my life to work, and this includes the behaviors and attitudes that I think are appropriate for our girls. So much time gets spent sowing to the natural desires of "normal," "just one quiet evening," "one dinner without a meltdown," "one day without a violent outburst," that we totally lose our focus on just *being* with our kids in the midst of their stuff, resulting in tired, worn out, and burned out parents who have nothing left to give because everything we've given has been in our own strength. What if there's another way?

What if "to live to please the Spirit" brought a different type of life? I think it does. When we give up our idea of what our family should look like, act like, and be like (especially in crisis), we gain a freedom to relax and let God be God. We gain the ability to please the Spirit by sowing things like love, joy, peace, patience, kindness, goodness, faithfulness, gentleness, and self-control. Operating in the fruits of the Spirit brings a totally different type of steadfastness than operating by the fruit of our flesh in selfishness ("I" want to be comfortable), jealousy (I wish my kids were more ____), and selfish ambition (I am going to be a successful parent). Do you see the difference? Many of our frustrations and most of our discontent rises from our own sinful desires to have our lives be within our control and go according to our plans.

Our lives are not our own. We've been bought with a price far greater than any we could pay for ourselves. It is not to comfort that this life of Christ is calling us; it's to something far greater—sacrifice. Laying down our own sinful nature to pick up the nature of the Spirit is the work of the Cross. This job called parenting is the hardest and most fulfilling that we will ever have the privilege of pursing. It's also the most tiring. From sleepless nights in infancy to sleepless nights in teen/young adulthood and every good, hard, joy-filled and tear-filled moment in between, it can wear you out and take you out, if you let it.

> **"Our lives are not our own. We've been bought with a price far greater than any we could pay for ourselves. It is not to comfort that this life of Christ is calling us; it's to something far greater—sacrifice."**

So, let us not grow weary *in doing good*!!! Even in crisis, don't stop sowing into your child, offering words of encouragement and operating in love with a gentle spirit and patience in their journey. *In due season you will reap a harvest of blessing if you don't give up!* There will come a day when the current season of crisis is over, I promise. When that day comes, my goal is that the relationship I have with my daughters is stronger, better, and more fulfilling than any of us could have imagined. That, to me, is a harvest of blessing! Don't grow weary and give up.

◆ ◆ ◆

Scripture Meditation: Take a few moments to read the following Scriptures. Allow the Holy Spirit to speak to your heart about each of them.

Isaiah 40:29-31 "He gives power to the weak and strength to the powerless. Even youths will become weak and tired, and young men will fall in exhaustion. But those who trust in the Lord will find new strength. They will soar high on wings like eagles. They will run and not grow weary. They will walk and not faint."

2 Thessalonians 3:13,16 "As for the rest of you, dear brothers and sisters, never get tired of doing good. Now may the Lord of peace himself give you his peace at all times and in every situation. The Lord be with you all."

Colossians 1:28b-29 MSG "We teach in a spirit of profound common sense so that we can bring each person to maturity. To be mature is to be basic. Christ! No more, no less. That's what I'm working so hard at day after day, year after year, doing my best with the energy God so generously gives me."

Romans 8:35, 37, 38 "Can anything ever separate us from Christ's love? Does it mean he no longer loves us if we have trouble or clarity, or are persecuted, or hungry, or destitute, or in danger, or threatened with death? No. Despite all these things, overwhelming victory is ours through Christ, who loved us. And I am convinced that nothing can every separate us from God's love. Neither death nor life, neither angels nor demons, neither our fears for today nor our worries about tomorrow—not even the powers of hell can separate us from God's love."

Capturing Thoughts: Throughout your adoption journey, I encourage you

to capture your thoughts, fears, moments of joy, memories, and challenges. It will be a great encouragement to go back and read what you've written before. Looking back, you'll be surprised how much you and your family grow through your experiences.

Prayer Starter: Lord, we know that nothing ever separates us from your love for us. Give us the strength to parent our children through every situation with the same patience, love and mercy that you parent us. Give us wisdom to know every good thing that would benefit, encourage and bring healing to our child, especially in this difficult time. Thank you for the energy that you so generously give us to parent and love well.

Discussion Questions – Day 27: Don't Grow Weary

1. Weariness sometimes sneaks up on us when we least expect it. Share when you first realized you were reaching the end of your rope in your parenting.

2. Isaiah 40:29-31 says, "Even youths will become weak and tired, and young men will fall in exhaustion." How does this portion of scripture encourage you? Read the entire passage again and write a message to yourself to read when you're tired and worn out. Share this message with your group.

3. What are some of the most fulfilling times in your relationships with your child? What are some of the most exhausting? Are there ways that you can do a better job at relaxing in the midst of the challenge?

4. Describe to the group what your hopes and dreams are for your relationship with your child in the future (a month from now, or even ten years from now). What can this group do to remind and support you in seeing that future come to pass?

My Journey:

(Use this space to capture your thoughts, prayers, concerns and questions)

...FOR ASSUREDLY, I SAY TO YOU, 'IF YOU HAVE FAITH AS A MUSTARD SEED, YOU WILL SAY TO THIS MOUNTAIN MOVE FROM HERE TO THERE, AND IT WILL MOVE; AND NOTHING WILL BE IMPOSSIBLE FOR YOU.'

MATTHEW 17:20

DAY 28: FAITH AS A MUSTARD SEED

The mustard seed is one of the tiniest seeds to plant yet it quickly becomes one of the largest and most robust plants/trees in the garden. Each of us, as followers of Jesus Christ, parents, spouses, friends, and fully functioning (mostly) adults, are trees in God's garden of life. Planted years ago as tiny infants, watered, cultivated and pruned by life and significant people along the way. Thousands of mustard seed faith moments have gotten both you and me here. For me, it's against all odds that not only would I be a devoted follower of Jesus, but a wife of nearly 25 years, mom to seven amazing daughters, and a voice in the parenting world for foster and adoptive parents. No really. Against all odds.

"Pam, you're a special girl." I hear the low, soft, and sweet voice of my Aunt Patsy saying these words to me. I'm five or six and have floated into her kitchen looking for something else to do. Bored with my brothers, bored with the coloring books and crayons that are always in the front room table, and done admiring the boxes of dress patterns lined up in her room. She offers me a slice of pie as my brothers run rampant around the pool table in the basement right below where we sit. The voices of my dad and uncle hum near us from the living room where they sit chomping on sunflower seeds and talking about cars, I guess. I never really listened. My Aunt Patsy always made me feel safe. Special. It's as if she saw some level of greatness in me that no one else could see. I don't know if she really saw it, or if she just understood the principle of seed faith in a deep way. Either way, she sowed faith into my life that I *was* different, special. Set apart. I believed her. This is one of the sweet profound memories of seed faith that I remember from my childhood.

Aunt Patsy was one of many people in my journey of life who sowed seeds of faith, little pieces of hope that led me to believe that I could be different. In her home, I could dream, relax, and be a kid. I was special, she said so. Avid church-goers, I'm convinced that not only did she sow seeds of faith into my life, she prayed them into existence. Alcohol, drugs—prescription and not, chaos, screaming, shouting, lying. So much lying. These were regular companions in my home. My parents married young and both battled their own demons within their marriage and in their personal lives. They did the best they knew how, I'm convinced of that. They loved us, we knew that too. Our little family of five wasn't the picture-perfect family though, and it was hard on everyone. It wasn't all bad; we had great memories too, like pizza Fridays, cheese-wiz and Ritz crackers, and summers by the lake.

One of the best things that my parents ever gave me was a love of reading. They were both readers, my dad loving westerns and my mom romance novels, the steamy kind. This, however, got me in trouble. Big, almost life-altering trouble. I picked up my first Harlequin at about age nine and became addicted. I graduated from Harlequin to the thicker books in my early teen years—they were much more exciting. "The talk" for me came really early and the giver of the talk was the authors of my mom's books, what I now know are best categorized as Erotica. Boy did they teach me a lot about how men and women were suppose to relate, what romance was all about, and what makes men tick. I learned it so well that I used it, word-for-word, on my ninth-grade boyfriend—straight out of the book. I wrote the scene word-for-word on college-ruled paper, folded it all cute and gave it to him on the bus. I had changed the names in the scene to ours and couldn't wait to see the satisfaction on his face as he realized all the possibilities of our budding relationship. Outside of the books, however, I had never even kissed a boy. Held hands, yes. Passed notes, yes. But, he didn't know that and I liked him. I wanted him to think I knew about relationships and how "real" relationships were supposed to be. I'm sure you can guess that this story has a very poor ending. It does. This particular boyfriend was also the son of our Pastor...the Pastor of our tiny Southern Baptist—everyone knows everyone and everyone has known everyone for generations—church in the middle of nowhere. Well, as fate would have it, the Pastor of our tiny Southern Baptist church finds this particular note in his son's dresser drawer one day. Yep.

The fact that I'm even here typing this nearly 30 years later is a water-into-wine miracle. I was forbidden from even giving "the boy" a passing glance from that point on and labeled a troublemaker. You can only imagine. Thank God we didn't have Facebook back then. No, really, thank God. Sexually promiscuous. Fast. Loose. These were all labels that were applied to me during this incident. I can only imagine the waging tongues of many and the raging speculation as to how worrisome my future would be. Truth be told, by all measures, that probably should have been, and easily could have been, my story. But it's not.

Instead my story is different. It's the story of all humanity—redemption, salvation, grace, and faith. Seed faith. Faith sown in pieces as small as mustard seeds by people all along my journey, some of whom spent hours on the phone with me, listening to the ramblings of a teenager, and teaching me my value. Others who loved me, despite my "stuff." Still more who poured into me along the way, as a wife, as a mother, as an employee, and as a friend. God calls some to plant, some to water, and others to reap; it's the journey of Christ-likeness for every single one of us. It's the journey of Christ-likeness for your kids, too, and mine.

> **"Dream big about the day that the harvest of righteousness is reaped in your child's life. It will be."**

As a battle-weary parent you might feel like the chance of things changing is so small that it's nearly impossible. Well, out of the mouth of Jesus himself, He assures you that faith, even like a mustard seed, is all you need. Nothing is impossible. Have faith to believe that the seeds you've sown will bear fruit, even if they're mustard seed-sized.

Have the audacity to pray those people into your children's life who will water what you've planted. Dream big about the day that the harvest of righteousness is reaped in your child's life. It will be. And like my Aunt Patsy, never lose a moment to look your child in the eye and say, "You're special."

◆ ◆ ◆

Scripture Meditation: Take a few moments to read the following Scriptures. Allow the Holy Spirit to speak to your heart about each of them.

Acts 20:35 "And I have been a constant example of how you can help those in need by working hard. You should remember the words of the Lord Jesus, 'It is more blessed to give than to receive'"

2 Corinthians 9:6-8 "Remember this—a farmer who plants only a few seeds will get a small crop. But the one who plants generously will get a generous crop. You must each decide in your heart how much to give. And don't give reluctantly or in response to pressure. For God loves a person who gives cheerfully. And God will generously provide all you need. Then you will always have everything you need and plenty left over to share with others."

Hebrews 11:1 "Faith is the confidence that what we hope for will actually happen; it gives us assurance about things we cannot see."

Matthew 21:21-22 "Then Jesus told them, 'I tell you the truth, if you have faith and don't doubt, you can do things like this and much more. You can even say to this mountain, 'May you be lifted up and thrown into the sea,' and it will happen. You can pray for anything, and if you have faith, you will receive it."

Capturing Thoughts: Throughout your adoption journey, I encourage you to capture your thoughts, fears, moments of joy, memories, and challenges. It will be a great encouragement to go back and read what you've written before. Looking back, you'll be surprised how much you and your family grow through your experiences.

Prayer Starter: Father, help us to see the greatness that you have planned for our children's lives. Help us to plant the seeds of purpose, confidence, and faith into their hearts. We also ask that you bring other people into our children's lives who will lead, guide, love, and point them toward you. We believe that even though we don't see everything we'd like to right now, you still have great plans for our children's lives and will draw them toward you throughout the course of their lives.

Discussion Questions – Day 28: Faith as a Mustard Seed

1. In today's devotion Pam shares a personal story about a major "behavior" in her freshman year of high school. If you had been the adults in this situation, how would you have interpreted Pam's behaviors? What would your fears/concerns have been? How would you have handled it?

2. Read 2 Corinthians 9:6-8. Consider the seeds of love, faith, and purpose that you're sowing into your child's life. Can you anticipate a small crop or an abundant crop? Take time to evaluate your own heart. Are you sowing willingly and cheerfully? Consider changes that you might make to improve in this area of your relationship with your child.

3. Like Pam's Aunt Patsy, do you have memories of people who've sown into your life from childhood until now? What impact have those seeds made on the person that you are today?

4. As a parent, are there areas you're struggling in your faith? Share ways this group can pray for you in this area.

My Journey:

(Use this space to capture your thoughts, prayers, concerns and questions)

For the law was given through Moses, but grace and truth came
through Jesus Christ.

John 1:17

DAY 29: GRACE & TRUTH

One of the most frequent questions that I hear from other parents when
discussing how to handle their child's behaviors is, "So, are you telling me
we're just supposed to let it all go and have *grace?*" That last word formed as
they draw their head back, snarl their nose, and give me that disapproving
and dismissive look of complete consternation. No. I'm telling you to have
grace alongside *truth.* There's a difference. Too often, especially as
'responsible' parents, we lean heavily on the side of truth (consequences,
edicts, lectures) without even a measure of grace (understanding). Other
times, especially as 'cool' parents, we lean heavily on the side of grace
without even a measure of truth. Jesus brought balance to the law of Moses
when He came to the earth. Until His arrival, there was law, and within it,
there was no escape from the judgment of the law except through sacrifice.
Jesus came and became the embodiment of the law, balancing it with grace
and truth.

The balance of grace and truth are described well in this quote from our
pastor, Dennis Rouse, "Grace and Truth are the foundation for all
followers of Christ to build from. When we emphasize one over the other,
it creates a shallow soil in our heart for God to produce fruit in. It seems
today that there is heavy emphasis on grace and a low emphasis on truth. I
thank God every day for His grace, but I'm pretty sure Jesus said it's the
truth that sets me free! I need *both*—the encouragement of grace balanced

with the correction of truth. All you have to do is look at what happens when a generation of children are raised by parents who over emphasize encouragement and under emphasize correction; the result of that tells you all you need to know about grace and truth." Without truth, there is no need for grace. Grace simply says, "I understand why you did this (immaturity, anger, distrust, deregulation, peer pressure, etc.)" while truth says, "Here's why what you did is not okay (broke trust, hurt someone else, is sinful, caused disorder, was rude, etc.)." Grace and truth combined make room for our children's imperfections and mistakes while also teaching them the truth about their behaviors and attitudes. As a parent, you absolutely must function in both.

In parenting, specifically Christian parenting, there are three sets of rules to which we teach our children to abide. The first is Biblical standards. These are nonnegotiable standards of behaviors and value systems universal to each of us as believers, regardless of our age—eight or eighty—as defined by the Bible. The second is the rules of our home. We each have a standard of behavior, attitude, and family functioning set within our homes. Yours will very likely differ from mine, and that's okay. The third is the set of rules that apply are those which are outside of our homes—in school, at work, and in general society. These change based on the environment and are just as important as the first two sets of rules. We have a responsibility to our children and to our society to teach our children healthy obedience and respect for the rules that exist in life. These rules (truths) are what they are, and we don't (for the most part) have the power to change them. It's good and healthy to teach our children that there are black and white truths that exist as believers, family members, and contributing members of society. We do this by telling them the truth and correcting their behaviors when they've broken a rule or encouraging their behavior when they've obeyed one. Having grace isn't about sugarcoating bad behavior. Actually, it's the opposite; to truly have grace is to deal with the bad behavior in a spirit of truth, seasoned with love.

Grace is a very misunderstood topic, especially in today's society. For the most part we believe that grace is the whitewashing of our failures, behaviors, and sins. Even Jesus' death on the cross, the ultimate measure of grace, didn't whitewash our sins; it magnified them by highlighting the truth that our sins could only be atoned for through death—His death on the cross, in our place. That's not a covering up of sin; it's sin's payment. Oh, how we've misrepresented and devalued the sacrifice of grace our Savior embodied on the Cross by turning grace into a license to sin. I'm so grateful for the saving grace that's been poured out on my behalf through the cross.

To have grace for our children in the midst of their behaviors is to teach and train them from a place of understanding. Understanding first, were it not for Jesus, our own sins and transgressions would be stacked up in judgment against us as a testimony to our imperfections and failures. Secondly, understanding that the process of sanctification is also a measure of grace and in all of us, it takes time. He who began a good work in your family *is* faithful to complete it. We learn and grow through failure and pain. Allow your children the freedom to make mistakes, to sin, to fail, to lie, and to behave badly without making it a personal attack on you. Rather, look at it through the lens of growth and have the sanctifying grace to be with them in the midst of failure and remind them that it's going to be okay, and they are experiencing growth through learning, just like we all do.

There are many types of grace poured out on us as believers and described within the Word. Two that we've talked about are *saving* grace and *sanctifying* grace. We should review a few other types of grace that we need to practice with our children, especially in crisis—provisional grace, sustaining grace, and abounding grace. Provisional grace provides for all of our needs, according to His riches in glory. This type of grace is always there, watching, providing, and caring for us, sometimes even in our darkest places. Providing for our children, even in crisis, is a privilege—food, clothing, and shelter are basic things (even if it's not within our home for a season) we can assure our children of because they belong to us. Sustaining grace lifts you up in times of trial and gives you the strength to endure, the wisdom to understand, and the faith to hope. It's this very grace that, as a battle-weary parent, you and I are holding onto in our darkest hours. It's also the grace that we should ask God to grant unwaveringly to our children, that even in their darkest hour He will sustain them, give them the strength to endure, the wisdom to understand, and the faith to hope for a better tomorrow. Finally, there is abounding grace, God's unmerited favor toward us. We have done nothing to earn it. He just simply loves on us because we are His. As His sons and daughters He delights in every aspect of our being, even when we're being very bad. Our children need to feel our abounding love toward them, the unmerited favor of being our child and the delight of our lives, even when they're being very bad.

The balance of grace and truth is the embodiment of our Savior Jesus

> **"As His sons and daughters He delights in every aspect of our being, even when we're being very bad. Our children need to feel our abounding love toward them, the unmerited favor of being our child and the delight of our lives, even when they're being very bad."**

Christ and His work on the cross for our salvation. Our homes should be filled with grace solidly balanced on a foundation of truth. This balance of structure and nurture produces the healthiest children and the calmest parents. We can't always stop our children from going off the rails and behaving badly, but we can stop ourselves from going off the rails with them. Stand firm, in love, as a trusted guardian of their heart and never stop seeing the potential of tomorrow.

Scripture Meditation: Take a few moments to read the following Scriptures. Allow the Holy Spirit to speak to your heart about each of them.

> **Psalms 119:160** "The very essence of your words is truth; all your just regulations will stand forever."

> **John 1:14** "So the Word became human and made his home among us. He was full of unfailing love and faithfulness. And we have seen his glory, the glory of the Father's one and only Son."

> **John 8:31** "Jesus said to the people who believed in him, 'You are truly my disciples if you remain faithful to my teachings. And you will know the truth, and the truth will set you free."

> **1 Peter 4:10 NIV** "Each of you should use whatever gift you have received to serve others, as faithful stewards of God's grace in its various forms."

Capturing Thoughts: Throughout your adoption journey, I encourage you to capture your thoughts, fears, moments of joy, memories, and challenges. It will be a great encouragement to go back and read what you've written before. Looking back, you'll be surprised how much you and your family grow through your experiences.

Prayer Starter: Jesus, thank you for coming on our behalf to balance truth with grace for us. Give us the ability to lead our home according to biblical standards. Enlarge our hearts with unfailing love toward our children as an example of your unfailing love for us. As we deal with difficult behaviors and crisis moments, allow us to walk in discernment and deal with bad behavior in a spirit of truth, seasoned with love.

Discussion Questions – Day 29: Grace & Truth

1. In your parenting, do you tend to lean heavily on either grace or truth without the balance of the other? Talk about your parenting style and how today's devotion challenges you.

2. In today's devotion, Pam says, "Having grace isn't about sugarcoating bad behavior. Actually, it's the opposite.; to truly have grace is to deal with the bad behavior in a spirit of truth, seasoned with love." Do you struggle with the idea of "grace," feeling like it's letting your kids off the hook? Talk about a recent disciplinary moment with your child. Discuss whether you could have delivered the truth (why what you did is not okay) and balanced it with grace (I understand why you did it).

3. Read 1 Peter 4:10 NIV. Pam talks about different types of grace throughout today's devotion. As faithful stewards of God's grace in its various forms, how do you feel today's devotion has challenged or encouraged you?

4. Have you found yourself having a hard time seeing the potential within your child to overcome? Talk about this with the group.

My Journey:

(Use this space to capture your thoughts, prayers, concerns and questions)

DO NOT REMEMBER THE FORMER THINGS, NOR CONSIDER THE THINGS OF OLD.

ISAIAH 43:18

DAY 30: FORGETTING THE PAST

We all know that we can't compare ourselves to the family down the street, but what we sometimes miss is that we can't compare ourselves to the family we "used to be" either. Many times in crisis we look back, and we wonder where the good times went. What happened to that sweet, adorable, and wonderful child we used to know? Not too long ago we were that picture-perfect family...where did that go? In the same way trying to be like the family down the street can become an idol in our life, so can trying to make things the way they were *before*. Before this child moved in. Before they went to high school. Before they had to go away to residential treatment. Before they ran away. Before they were violent towards us. Before. It's an idol whose hold we must break on our lives if we're going to move forward in healing as a family, or as individuals.

> "We all know that we can't compare ourselves to the family down the street, but what we sometimes miss is that we can't compare ourselves to the family we "used to be" either."

Recently I attended The Refresh Conference near Seattle, Washington. Refresh is an outreach of the orphan ministry at Overlake Christian Church and is run by dear friends of mine, Andrew & Michele Schneidler. The whole goal of the conference is to provide foster and adoptive families with much needed refreshment while allowing

194

them to get all of their training hours in one place. The atmosphere is like no other conference I've attended; it truly is all about loving on and caring for—deeply caring for—these families who are in the trenches with wounded and hurting children. After one of the evening sessions of the conference, they did one of the most powerful exercises that I've ever had the privilege of being a part of, the plate exercise. I loved it so much that I've included it as supplemental material at the end of this book. The purpose of the exercise is to take a beautiful plate that represents the *old life* you had before this crisis entered your life. On the beauty of the plate, write the things that have stolen that life from you. After it's written on, throw it as hard as you can and break it. From there, you walk away into a *new life* putting the old behind you and cleansing yourself of the clutch of the enemy who's stealing your life and joy in the present. I cannot properly describe what was like to watch thousands of men and women, tears streaming down their faces, throw plates into a hole to break them. As their plates shattered at the bottom, they honestly *felt* free for the first time in a long time. Written on the shards of glass covering the bottom of the hole were words like these: *suicide, depression, violent outbursts, lying, wetting the bed, divorce, bitterness, resentment, hatred, exhaustion, sexual abuse, anxiety, sleeplessness, and so so so many more.* The level of pain that existed in that room, the sheer amount of sorrow and sacrifice among these families nearly did me in. It was by far the most profound image of laying aside the former things in our lives that I've ever personally experienced.

Our Jesus is BIG, and He loves BIG. As tears streamed down my own face, I physically watched freedom, healing, and deliverance happen. Marriages were restored, depression healed, strength restored; this, my friends, is how we win when we're battle-weary—arm-in-arm with one another, covered in the grace and love of our Jesus. Don't miss reading Andrew & Michele's letter in the next pages of this book; you will be forever changed.

In order to move forward, we absolutely must heed these words from Isaiah, *"do not remember the former things, nor consider the things of old."* It can be difficult to accept what might be our new normal in family life, but for a season, that's exactly what you have to do in order to gain the refreshment of the Lord in the midst of trial. In accepting the new normal, let me encourage you to bring back some of the joy that may have seeped out of the household, one bad behavior at a time. Family game night. A trip to the movies. Fun in the park. Love, laughter, and family unity. I know it's hard, and it may even feel like a reward for bad behavior, but nothing—nothing—rebuilds broken relational walls like a good old-fashioned belly laugh and a shared memory. Get out the board games, dust off the deck of cards, and have a little fun. You'll be thankful that you did, and you'll discover that the new memories that you're building are better and more richly rewarding than the ones *before*.

Even though the storm clouds are right above you, the storm is brewing all around you, and the thunder claps are drowning out the sounds of joy that used to define your life, for just a moment, put down your umbrella, stretch your hands toward the sky, and dance with abandon in the rain. Every single moment, from this moment on, remember that you are not alone or without hope. His mercies are new every single morning, *ready or not*.

Scripture Meditation: Take a few moments to read the following Scriptures. Allow the Holy Spirit to speak to your heart about each of them.

Isaiah 61:2 & 3 "He has sent me to tell those who mourn that the time of the Lord's favor has come, and with it, the day of God's anger against their enemies. To all who mourn in Israel, he will give a crown of beauty for ashes, a joyous blessing instead of mourning, festive praise instead of despair. In their righteousness, they will be like great oaks that the Lord has planted for his own glory."

Philippians 3:13-14 "No, dear brothers and sisters, I have not achieved it, but I focus on this one thing; forgetting the past and looking forward to what lies ahead, I press on to reach the end of the race and receive the heavenly prize for which God, through Christ Jesus, is calling us."

Ephesians 4:31-32 "Get rid of all bitterness, rage, anger, harsh words, and slander, as well as all types of evil behavior. Instead be kind to each other, tenderhearted, forgiving one another, just as God through Christ has forgiven you."

Hebrews 10:17-18 "Then he says, 'I will never again remember their sins and lawless deeds'. And when sins have been forgiven, there is no need to offer any more sacrifices."

Capturing Thoughts: Throughout your adoption journey, I encourage you to capture your thoughts, fears, moments of joy, memories, and challenges. It will be a great encouragement to go back and read what you've written before. Looking back, you'll be surprised how much you and your family grow through your experiences.

Prayer Starter: Lord, help us to forget the past and let go of any bitterness or unforgiveness that we might be holding in our heart. Thank you for renewing our strength and granting us the ability to move forward, even in the midst of the storm. Help us to discover the joy in every moment and to relax in our trust of you in difficult times. We are grateful for a future full of hope that you've given us through your sacrifice on our behalf

Discussion Questions – Day 30: Forgetting the Past

1. Do you find it hard to let go of things that have happened in the past? Are there still behaviors you hold onto? Talk about why it's so difficult for you to let go.

2. Read Philippians 3:13-14. How does this scripture challenge or encourage you?

3. Pam closes this devotional study with this statement, "Every single moment, from this moment on, remember that you are not alone or without hope. His mercies are new every single morning, *ready or not.*" What are some ways that you can remind yourself of this when you're in a moment of crisis or battle-weariness?

4. Talk about ways this group can support you as you continue your journey forward with your children.

My Journey:

(Use this space to capture your thoughts, prayers, concerns and questions)

THE PLATE EXERCISE

As experienced at The Refresh Conference 2015

You will need:

- One large ceramic dinner plate (avoid glass or "Corelle" type of products)
- Black permanent felt-tipped pen
- Safety goggles

You will receive:

- HOPE for your future.
- Cathartic release
- A way through your wilderness.
- Streams in your wasteland.

As parents, all of us have a story. In our stories, we have events that occurred in our past, in our present, and will occur in our future. Some are good, and some are bad. And for some of us, if we were to count up the events in our lives, it would seem the bad outweigh the good. **But the question is: which events are we holding on to?**

Isaiah 43:18-19 (NIV) says **"Forget the former things; do not dwell on the past. See, I am doing a new thing! Now it springs up; do you not perceive it? I am making a way in the wilderness and streams in the wasteland."**

"Former things" are life experiences that have occurred in our past. You'll notice Isaiah does not say *"Pretend your past never occurred. Don't talk about it.*

Just move on." No. **It's not wrong to acknowledge our past – even the painful parts like hurts or broken dreams. But we are warned not to <u>dwell</u> on the past.** Why not?

Isaiah tells us the answer: if we are stuck looking in reverse -- dwelling on the *past* -- we are likely to miss the great things God is doing in our *present*. God is doing a new thing right now, but we have to see it, and we won't see it if our eyes are glued to our rear-view mirrors.

Some of you might be reading this and thinking, *"Have you seen my life? My life is a mess. My kids are a wreck. My marriage is a wreck. I am a wreck. What I am living through right now is hard. Really, really hard."*

Isaiah is not saying the key to life is a quick-fix, superficial positive attitude. Nor does he promise a change to our circumstances. The truth is a faith-filled adventure in a fallen world is neither simplistic nor risk-free. In fact, **Isaiah warns our journey runs us headlong into wilderness. And** *wasteland.*

Wait. What??

But don't miss two key words in the passage: "way" and "streams." If we can let go of our former things and quit dwelling on the past, God assures us: *"there will be wilderness ahead, but I will make a WAY through it for you. And your journey may also cross through wasteland, but don't be afraid. I will give you STREAMS to sustain you while you make it through."* Regardless of whether our circumstances change, **when we stop dwelling on our past and instead look forward to perceive what God is doing around us, there is HOPE!**

So this takes us back to the opening question: what former things are you holding on to today? When your hand clasps around an object, your hand is closed. **That means you cannot let go of the object, but also means you cannot receive something new.**

What prior hurt or experience do you need to let go of? A mistake? A betrayal? Bitterness? Difficulty forgiving others? Yourself? Or, maybe it's not a bad thing. Do you feel called to a change in your life that seems risky? Do you feel drawn to this calling, but are held back in pursuing it because *for once, life has finally calmed down and life is finally easy?*

Could it be God has so much more waiting for you, if you would just let go of your former things? Are you willing to trust God to make a way through the wilderness? To give you streams in the wastelands that lay ahead?

Make a mental list of the things you are still holding on to. The good, the bad, the ugly. Maybe it is shame from long ago. Or resentment as you struggle to meet someone else's unhealthy expectations of you? Maybe your fist is still clenched around unrealistic expectations you set on being the perfect parent? *If you could learn this parenting style better, then you'd fix your kid. If you could read more parenting books or blogs, then you could fix your family. Fix your marriage. Fix yourself.*

When you have completed your list, go purchase the largest ceramic dinner plate you can find. With a permanent felt-tipped pen, write down the "former things" you are still holding on to but want to let go of. Perhaps your list is so long you'll need two plates. Or a dinner platter! No matter. Keep writing until you have them all down.

When finished, put on your safety goggles and take your plates to a place with a large open hard surface. A parking lot, an empty fireplace, a back patio. You may find this part of the exercise to be difficult, but when you are ready, pray this prayer and throw the plates as HARD as you can: *"God! I am tired of dwelling on the past. I don't want to miss the way you are making for me through this wilderness! I need your springs in this wasteland! I forever give you these former things, God. Please take them from me. They are yours, God. I'm not taking them back!!"*

Now THROW!

Throw your plate like you've never thrown anything before. Perhaps you need to scream when you throw. Perhaps you are laughing. Perhaps sobbing. When we did this at The Refresh Conference, many people clung to spouses or close friends for strength before finally letting go of that persistent former thing that had held them captive for so long. Whatever it is, throw the plate with all your might and then enjoy the glorious sight & sounds while it shatters into a thousand pieces.

With your phone, take a picture of the shards of plate at your feet.

No more.

No more will you dwell on the past. At your feet lay one thousand reasons why you will now perceive what God is doing around you.

If you ever start to dwell on the former things again, take out that picture and remember: **He will make a *way* through your wilderness and give you *streams* in the wasteland.** He is always with you and He is always faithful.

You can do this. And remember, you can always go buy another plate. ☺

Andrew & Michele Schneidler

therefreshconference.org

AFTERWORD

In the early years of our adoptions I thought adoption was all about the children— about their healing, their restoration, their destiny. And indeed the extravagant love of Father God for our children through adoption still leaves me stunned, awed by who this God is, and humbled that He would invite me into such a beautiful and powerful expression of His heart. But as the years have gone by I have also found myself stunned by the pain of my children, swirling fears and deep wounds that find expression in hurtful words and destructive actions. And it is through these struggles that God has whispered to me that His purposes are as stunningly glorious and extravagant for us parents as is His love for the orphan.

As I read Pam's devotional for the Battle-Weary Parent I had the wonderful, though slightly disturbing feeling that she had been living in my home, or at least had peeked through our windows on and off over the past 15 years. And I suspect many of you experienced the same as you read this gift of a book. That God placed this book in Pam's heart is clear to me. That she shares from real-life rubber-meets-the-road experience is also clear, and works as a balm to my soul. That she speaks truth and hope in each chapter, tenderly calling me back to truth and infusing me with fresh hope, is also very clear.

The truths Pam shares are ones you and I need to go back and feed from over and over in this long-haul journey that is adoption and foster care. What a gift to us parents to have access to these bite-sized dishes of goodness! It is God's nature to provide for us abundantly and without cost, and I believe this devotional is a wonderful offering on His table for you and me. For I have found it to be true that when I focus on my child and his/her needs and issues I am indeed a battle-weary mother. But when I eat from this table, freely set for me, without regard for my performance today as an adoptive or foster parent, but based solely on God's grace, the work of His Son on my behalf, I am strengthened and ready to once again love without condition.

Over and over Pam brings home the life-giving point that it is never too late to grow as parents. And that is where I want to leave us, standing with anticipation at the doorway to growth and change. Not my child's growth, but mine and yours! May these devotionals expand us all, not simply by our reading and discussing them with friends, but by our willingness to try new approaches, to ask our children for forgiveness when we fail, to hope once again in His never-failing love---and to let the Spirit of God shape us into the stunningly beautiful shape that is adoption!

So dear ones, let us live as beloved sons and daughters of our Daddy God so that when we are battle-weary and have used up all the love and patience and parenting wisdom in our arsenal, we reach out to receive from the One who gives generously to us, without finding fault or making accusations. The best mothers and fathers are first daughters and sons!

Let the parenting wisdom in this devotional influence you, let the hope infuse you, let the truth reshape you, let the presence of the Father change you as you co-labor with Him in this beautiful work that is adoption and fostering. May the trajectory of your life and the life of your child be ever changed!

Beth Templeton

hopeathome.org

ABOUT THE AUTHOR

Pam Parish is the president and founder of Connections Homes, an Atlanta-based nonprofit organization focused on providing family-based home environments where adolescents with difficult pasts and uncertain futures can connect, grow and belong. She and her husband, Steve, were high school sweethearts. More than two decades later, they are still best friends. At the time of this writing, they have seven daughters and one son-in-law: Katya Grace, Kelsey Joy, Elizabeth Yeaune Harang (Jesus' blessing and love), Tyree James & Seara Serenity, Charlie Selah, Kristan Faith, and Heather Hope. They also have three grandsons, Juan, Jayden and Junior, and one granddaughter, Adrianna. Pam is a foster care and adoption advocate, public speaker, trainer, and family crisis mentor.

Ready or Not for Families Growing Through Foster Care & Adoption

Book One in the Ready or Not Series for Foster and Adoptive Families

Entering the journey of foster care and adoption can be one of the most daunting decisions that you make as a parent. Parenting a child who has experienced trauma and loss is a rewarding experience, but it's not easy.

In this biblically-centered and straight-forward book, Pam Parish helps parents to:

- Consider the impact of foster care and adoption on their lives and families.

- Evaluate their motives and expectations for the foster care and adoption experience.

- Explore foster care and adoption through the lens of scripture.

To stay up-to-date on the *Ready or Not Series* visit <u>readyornotresources.com</u>

Family Photo Credit: Kelly Hopkins

Connect With Pam Online

@pamparish

facebook.com/pamparish

pinterest.com/pamparish

google.com/+pamparish

Pam also shares inspiration for foster and adoptive parents on her blog: **pamparish.com**.

To inquire about having Pam speak at your church, agency or conference e-mail booking@pamparish.com or visit pamparish.com/contact.

Scripture has much to say about about orphans. Here's a list of verses that mention the fatherless and orphan.

Exodus 22:22-24

Do not take advantage of a widow or an **orphan**. If you do and they cry out to me, I will certainly hear their cry. My anger will be aroused, and I will kill you with the sword; your wives will become widows and your children **fatherless**.

Deuteronomy 10:18

He defends the cause of the **fatherless** and the widow, and loves the alien, giving him food and clothing.

Deuteronomy 14:29

So that the Levites (who have no allotment or inheritance of their own) and the aliens, the **fatherless** and the widows who live in your towns may come and eat and be satisfied, and so that the LORD your God may bless you in all the work of your hands.

Deuteronomy 16:11

And rejoice before the LORD your God at the place he will choose as a dwelling for his Name—you, your sons and daughters, your menservants and maidservants, the Levites in your towns, and the aliens, the **fatherless** and the widows living among you.

Deuteronomy 16:14

Be joyful at your Feast--you, your sons and daughters, your menservants and maidservants, and the Levites, the aliens, the **fatherless** and the widows who live in your towns.

Deuteronomy 24:17

Do not deprive the alien or the **fatherless** of justice, or take the cloak of the widow as a pledge.

Deuteronomy 24:19-21

When you are harvesting in your field and you overlook a sheaf, do not go back to get it. Leave it for the alien, the **fatherless** and the widow, so that the LORD your God may bless you in all the work of your hands. When you beat the olives from your trees, do not go over the branches a second time. Leave what remains for the alien, the **fatherless** and the widow. When you harvest the grapes in your vineyard, do not go over the vines again. Leave what remains for the alien, the **fatherless** and the widow.

Deuteronomy 26:12 -13

When you have finished setting aside a tenth of all your produce in the third year, the year of the tithe, you shall give it to the Levite, the alien, the **fatherless** and the widow, so that they may eat in your towns and be satisfied. Then say to the LORD your God: "I have removed from my house the sacred portion and have given it to the Levite, the alien, the **fatherless** and the widow, according to all you commanded. I have not turned aside from your commands nor have I forgotten any of them.

Deuteronomy 27:19

"Cursed is the man who withholds justice from the alien, the **fatherless** or the widow." Then all the people shall say, "Amen!"

Job 6:27

You would even cast lots for the **fatherless** and barter away your friend.

Job 22:7-11

You gave no water to the weary and you withheld food from the hungry, though you were a powerful man, owning land-- an honored man, living on it. And you sent widows away empty-handed and broke the strength of the **fatherless**. That is why snares are all around you, why sudden peril terrifies you, why it is so dark you cannot see, and why a flood of water covers you.

Job 24:2-4

Men move boundary stones; they pasture flocks they have stolen. They drive away the **orphan's** donkey and take the widow's ox in pledge. They thrust the needy from the path and force all the poor of the land into hiding.

Job 24:9

The **fatherless** child is snatched from the breast; the infant of the poor is seized for a debt.

Job 29:11-12

Whoever heard me spoke well of me, and those who saw me commended me, because I rescued the poor who cried for help, and the **fatherless** who had none to assist him.

Job 31:16-18

"If I have denied the desires of the poor or let the eyes of the widow grow weary, if I have kept my bread to myself, not sharing it with the **fatherless** - but from my youth I reared him as would a father, and from my birth I guided the widow.

Job 31:21-22

If I have raised my hand against the **fatherless**, knowing that I had influence in court, then let my arm fall from the shoulder, let it be broken off at the joint.

Psalm 10:14

But you, O God, do see trouble and grief; you consider it to take it in hand. The victim commits himself to you; you are the helper of the **fatherless**.

Psalm 10:17-18

You hear, O LORD, the desire of the afflicted; you encourage them, and you listen to their cry, defending the **fatherless** and the oppressed, in order that man, who is of the earth, may terrify no more.

Psalm 68:5-6

A father to the **fatherless**, a defender of widows, is God in his holy dwelling. God sets the lonely in families, he leads forth the prisoners with singing; but the rebellious live in a sun-scorched land.

Psalm 82:3-4

Defend the cause of the weak and **fatherless**; maintain the rights of the poor and oppressed. Rescue the weak and needy; deliver them from the hand of the wicked.

Psalm 94:6

They slay the widow and the alien; they murder the **fatherless**.

Psalm 146:9

The LORD watches over the alien and sustains the **fatherless** and the widow, but he frustrates the ways of the wicked.

Proverbs 23:10-11

Do not move an ancient boundary stone or encroach on the fields of the **fatherless**, for their Defender is strong; he will take up their case against you.

Isaiah 1:17

Learn to do right! Seek justice, encourage the oppressed. Defend the cause of the **fatherless**, plead the case of the widow.

Isaiah 1:23

Our rulers are rebels, companions of thieves; they all love bribes and chase after gifts. They do not defend the cause of the **fatherless**; the widow's case does not come before them.

Isaiah 9:17

Therefore the Lord will take no pleasure in the young men, nor will he pity the **fatherless** and widows, for everyone is ungodly and wicked, every mouth speaks vileness. Yet for all this, his anger is not turned away, his hand is still upraised.

Isaiah 10:1-2

Woe to those who make unjust laws, to those who issue oppressive decrees, to deprive the poor of their rights and withhold justice from the oppressed of my people, making widows their prey and robbing the **fatherless**.

Jeremiah 5:27-29

Like cages full of birds, their houses are full of deceit; they have become rich and powerful and have grown fat and sleek. Their evil deeds have no limit; they do not plead the case of the **fatherless** to win it, they do not defend the rights of the poor. Should I not punish them for this?" declares the LORD. "Should I not avenge myself on such a nation as this?"

Jeremiah 7:5-7

If you really change your ways and your actions and deal with each other justly, if you do not oppress the alien, the **fatherless** or the widow and do not shed innocent blood in this place, and if you do not follow other gods to your own harm, then I will let you live in this place, in the land I gave your forefathers for ever and ever.

Jeremiah 22:3

This is what the LORD says: Do what is just and right. Rescue from the hand of his oppressor the one who has been robbed. Do no wrong or violence to the alien, the **fatherless** or the widow, and do not shed innocent blood in this place.

Jeremiah 49:11

Leave your **orphans**; I will protect their lives. Your widows too can trust in me.

Ezekiel 22:7

In you they have treated father and mother with contempt; in you they have oppressed the alien and mistreated the **fatherless** and the widow.

Hosea 14:3

Assyria cannot save us; we will not mount war-horses. We will never again say 'Our gods' to what our own hands have made, for in you the **fatherless** find compassion.

Zechariah 7:10

Do not oppress the widow or the **fatherless**, the alien or the poor. In your hearts do not think evil of each other.

Malachi 3:5

So I will come near to you for judgment. I will be quick to testify against sorcerers, adulterers and perjurers, against those who defraud laborers of their wages, who oppress the widows and the **fatherless**, and deprive aliens of justice, but do not fear me," says the LORD Almighty.

John 14:18

I will not leave you as **orphans**; I will come to you.

James 1:27

Religion that God our Father accepts as pure and faultless is this: to look after **orphans** and widows in their distress and to keep oneself from being polluted by the world.

Made in the USA
Lexington, KY
31 March 2018